RADICALLY
Aligned

Vicki Chisholm

Before you dive into this book, let's get connected. Being in business is all about relationships afterall. Scan the QR codes below and let me keep up to date with your journey. My mission is your success!

FACEBOOK   LINKEDIN   INSTAGRAM

Copyright © 2024 Vicki Chisholm

Table of Contents

Introduction v

A little dedication, with love viii

CHAPTER 1:
Your Mindset & Energy Do Matter 1

CHAPTER 2:
Getting aligned with the Law of Attraction 14

CHAPTER 3:
Being Specific... Soul aligned intentions are K EY!............. 26

CHAPTER 4:
Getting Clarity: Who, What, Where and When 36

CHAPTER 5:
Your Money Mindset, Pricing and Overcoming Blocks 49

CHAPTER 6:
Understanding soul wounds & how they impact your business life and sabotage your dreams!................................ 64

CHAPTER 7:
Your Inner Rebel Marketing 77

CHAPTER 8:
Unlock Abundant Sales Your Way 95

CHAPTER 9:
Being Magnetic, Planning and Action 106

CHAPTER 10:
Committing to Your Success 118

CHAPTER 11:
Fast Track Your Way To Success 129

Final Thoughts 138

Introduction

The next action you take will be a nice long deep breath and… 1…2…3… exhale.

Now, let's repeat that 3 times more.

Feels good being able to just simply take a deep breath, right?! You'll be surprised how often deep breaths are forgotten. Yet they are so powerful to bring you back into the present moment and re-establish balance between mind and body.

Now that you have taken some deep breaths, are you ready to finally learn how to unlock your inner rebel and give yourself permission to have all that you desire?

I can hear you screaming "YES YES YES - I want it all Vicki!"

This is your space and time to create your next level of success—shall we get started?

There was a moment in time when I would have said this isn't possible. I was just 29, when my whole world was about to change after 12 years. I had 3 children, chronic fatigue, a business, an autoimmune disease; I was burnt out and functioning daily on fight/flight and autopilot.

Sounds familiar? Let's say goodbye and move on from that. Inside this book, you will learn how I overcame what the doctors said I wouldn't, all while transforming my life and business.

I learnt how to craft my £10ph into a six-figure business. I also learnt the hard way what not to do in business… and who not to listen to…

Over the years, since I decided to change my life, I have invested thousands, reclaimed my health, discovered what happiness means for me and also created a new way of being. In 2015, I became homeless with my children as I left an abusive and coercively controlling relationship. This was the moment I decided my life was going to change. I will forever be grateful for friends and family who took me and my children in. It was due to this support that I was able to navigate the challenges of homelessness, raising my children, co-parenting with someone who had traumatised me for years and running my business. I was determined to move on and create a different life for myself.

Unfortunately, in 2017, following a stint of burnout, I had to reclaim my power and find a new way to do life.

Doctors had told me to expect to be wheelchair-bound by the time I was 40. However, I decided against that option and opened up my mind to finding another way to survive. It was at that point my journey with energy psychology began... then reiki, then life coaching and by 2019, I was free from autoimmune disease, depression, anxiety and so much more.

But I still wasn't fully content. I had to go on a journey with my business to establish what radically aligned life and business meant for me. Which brings me here in 2024, publishing this book for you.

Radically Aligned in life and business is not just a one-time movement, it's a consistent action that brings joy, love, gratitude and acceptance to every area of your life.

Are you truly ready for radical alignment in your life and business? Are you willing to create soul aligned success?

Let's get started and discover more about you on this journey to success, and creating global impact, the radically aligned way to business and life.

A little dedication, with love

This book is dedicated to all spiritual entrepreneurs out there who are feeling ready to activate soul aligned success in life and business. Who have that deep 'knowing' inside that they are meant for more and can't quite pinpoint why they aren't reaching their goals yet.

I also write this book on behalf of my children: Jessica, Jasmine and Jade. I hope one day they will read this book and follow my path to follow their soul calling, unleash their gifts, and allow their spirit to unfold. I hope they can follow their heart, achieve more than they ever felt possible and create a world where life is what you make it.

Without these three amazing girls, this book, my life and my business wouldn't have unfolded in the way it has. May this book bring strength, hope, empowerment and joy to all who it may reach, all over the world.

CHAPTER 1

Your Mindset & Energy Do Matter

Running a business is a self-development process. You cannot grow your business if you are not prepared to grow yourself—this I believe to be fact. My story is the reason I believe this to be true; if I didn't start my own business, I wouldn't have been taken to a new path of hope and possibilities. I would have remained stuck living a life that would never have been mine.

What do you believe? Do you believe that running a business or wanting more for yourself is a self-development process?

Before we dive in any further (I tend to waffle sometimes when I'm passionate about something!), I want to make sure you are reading this book with the right intention. I'm not here to tell you what to think or how to act; instead, this book is written by me with love to help you unlock your own magnetic abundant success, your way!

Get your thinking cap on and turn those thoughts inwards because we are going to have fun here.

Do you truly believe that to grow a business you must grow yourself? Or do you have other thoughts on this? If you do, please write them down as I'd love you to share these with me later.

In 2013, my first ever business coach, Rachel Stone, invited me to her workshop to plan my best year yet. I'd never done anything like this before: I was always the 'let's dive in and wing it style achiever'.

Although it was a few years ago now, I remember sitting there, tapping the pencils on the table and thinking I didn't know how to answer these questions. The questions were simple; I remember Rachel saying to me: "Dream big Vicki. Go to 10 years from now. What do you want for your life, your family, your business?" It took me ages to be able to open my mind to a bigger dream, I could barely see past the end of the week. I had always lived in survival mode, not dreamland!

I was a massively ambitious and driven woman, knowing what I wanted for my business was easy but knowing what I wanted for myself was something else entirely. As we began to unpick the logic and I got out of my own way, I had an idea: I wanted to be able to travel the world with my children and show them the infinite possibilities of what the world had to offer them. I drew a plane, closed my eyes, visualised being on that plane, with a nanny and tutor. For the very first time in my life, I was dreaming BIG.

> *EXERCISE:* Now it's your turn to dream big. Tune into your heart space and ask yourself where you want to be in 10 years, who you want to be and what do you want for your life, business, family… The deeper you can go with this, the better.

QUICK TIP: Place your hands on your heart and close your eyes. As you focus on your breath, repeat the questions. Visualise, feel, believe: take your mind to a place where there are no limits or fear — just possibilities. DREAM BIG!

(Make a note of the date and your dream as you will want to come back to this later).

Sometimes there is a blank void in our minds that stops us from seeing, feeling or believing in a dream. If you have experienced this, release any panic or frustration, and try the exercise again the next time you are in a relaxed space.

Resistance is futile, and I have officially labeled myself as the RESISTANCE QUEEN. If there is resistance to be had, I can assure you that I've felt it, experienced it and often got trapped inside of it. You can be rest assured though that resistance isn't all bad, it's just a part of your subconscious brain trying to keep you safe from emotional pain. You'll move through it in time. Be kind to yourself because it's okay to not be in the zone all the time.

Whilst we are on the topic of the subconscious mind, has there ever been a time when you were trying your best to implement change and do something new but found yourself sabotaging your success at every corner?

"F*CK the diets!" I used to say in complete horror.. "Forget it. There's no way in a million years I can diet, control my food intake, not have chocolate, cake, sweets, crisps or, dare I say it… CHIPS from the chip shop on the beach."

I was just not open to healthy eating or any change for that matter as it was all too scary. My mindset was one of lack and scarcity; I had been deprived of so much in my life, so changing my relationship with food was not about the next thing on my list. Instead, it was a form of sabotage. What I didn't see was that my energy was stuck in unworthiness. It wasn't ready to open to being worthy of healthy food and a better body. I was stuck in subconscious fear.

So, how do you recognise subconscious fear?

This is where the habits you've always had start to change. Some people live in fear their whole lives without even knowing it.

Take note: You don't have to be like them. You can be something brand new in your world and change the ancestral and generational lineage you may be carrying... This is the true power that lies within you.

Subconscious fears show up every single day, in common and uncommon ways. Here is one example that will impact your life and business every time you try to reach a new goal or change your life:

Imposter Syndrome: The subconscious fear that feeds you stories of not being good enough, smart enough, skinny enough, strong enough, pretty enough, tall enough, perfect enough or rich enough. These are ALL LIES!

*This list is not exhaustive.

Why does your subconscious feed you so many lies? The truth here is that the EGO (AKA the Subconscious) wants to keep you safe from emotional pain. The ego believes it's doing a good job by preventing you from revisiting past traumas and having feelings of shame, guilt, embarrassment and negative consequences. Sometimes these fears will show up and be totally illogical. Other times, they will feel so real it will feel like your chest is being crushed.

THE EGO: To understand your ego is to fall in love with safety and stability. The ego serves a purpose — to keep you safe when your life is being threatened. Think about being chased by a bear: if the bear catches you, you are one tasty meal to that bear. In this case, your ego is triggered into flight/fight mode, sending signals to the amygdala, a part of the brain that processes emotion and sends signals to release the stress hormone, cortisol. Cortisol, the stress hormone, is pumped around your body, increasing your heart rate and giving you the energy to get out of trouble.

As you can see, the ego serves its purpose to keep you safe. BUT... the ego also wants you to stay safe by not taking ANY RISKS at all.

What makes the ego become more and more afraid of you living your life? The simple answer is unhealed trauma, which is a subconscious fear that presents itself in many different scenarios.

Let me go back to the diet story... The days when I tried to lose weight and found myself gaining weight profusely was because my subconscious was feeding me lies, like:

"If I'm fat, ugly and unworthy.

However, I decided I was not going to be abused anymore. This fear was real but I didn't know I was carrying it until I did healing and energy work. As I began to unravel this story in my subconscious mind, I was suddenly very aware as to why I didn't want to be seen as an attractive woman. Childhood sexual abuse had led me to believe that if I was beautiful and attractive then I would be abused.

The more I unraveled this story, the more my life began to make sense to me. When I was in an abusive relationship, all he ever wanted me to wear were clothes he felt that I would look good in: skirts and tights, figure-hugging clothes and 'easy access' clothes. I distinctly remember saying to myself:

> "I'll wear trousers today; he won't be bugging me if I'm not attractive."

I spent years of my life hiding behind unattractive clothes to avoid unwanted attention. The effect of these traumas began showing up in my business and this was when it got real!

As you read this, I know part of you would be able to remember one point or another when you attempted to change who you are to stay safe and avoid any further trauma or drama. This is the ego in full alert.

When I discovered where my mind was, I was able to connect to the trauma energy that was trapped in my body. I could live my life free from past pain. My next job was to completely clear the energy.

Do you know what energy is? Some people do and some people don't. We will explore what it is, now.

Do you remember I said I had an autoimmune disease? It is fibromyalgia—the chronic disease that the doctors told me I would never recover from. My GP's exact words at the time were: "Go and find ways to cope with the pain; there's nothing more we can do for you."

I walked out of that GP's surgery that day and vowed to NEVER be a victim to fibromyalgia. I wholeheartedly believed there had to be another way. My mind was focused on my children. They didn't deserve a mum in this state, so I didn't plan to live the rest of my life like this.

I had a similar situation with a psychotherapist's office; after 16 weeks of therapy and nothing changed, I felt exactly the same walking into those offices as I did walking out. I burst into tears and said, "No, I won't live my life like this."

These were just two of the moments where I decided to change the script. It was my mindset that decided I needed to create change. But it was the next steps that changed my mindset all together.

Something I had to learn the hard way was that while saying what I wanted was easy, it wasn't as easy to maintain those thoughts. Especially when I had an abundance of self-doubt. It was at that point when I discovered the real meaning of energy.

Another fab piece of learning for you today:

Mindset is not everything... ENERGY IS.

Energy is the catalyst of the mind. When you are holding energy filled with emotion/trauma/memories/generational beliefs and ancestral baggage, it will naturally feed your mind.

The ego responds to the fears and emotions you store in your body. Which ultimately is an energy. The energy you feel inside is then feeding the brain thoughts, this is what I refer to as somatic healing. What you feel in your body is an energy that reflects to you what is happening inside.

Fibromyalgia symptoms, in my experience, would increase when I was stressed. The flare ups would be unexplainable and sometimes so horrific I couldn't cut a cucumber or turn my head. Other times, having a duvet on my lap over my knees was too painful and other times I'd be running around the house, dancing and completely pain free. However, none of it made any logical sense. One day I would be in good health and the next would feel like I had been hit by a train.

Disclaimer; my viewpoints and experience are not for medical advice/treatments. It's important you ascertain your own recovery journey with your GP.

The flareups often felt out of my control, UNTIL I learnt EFT – Emotional Freedom Technique, and energy psychology tool that rewires the brain using the meridian points on your body. I studied long and hard for days, weeks, months and years. After just 2 years of learning and daily implementation of EFT, I was free from fibromyalgia symptoms.

You are probably thinking how was this possible ... Well, I connected to the pain in my body and with my mentor's support, help and guidance, I was able to release the energy of trauma and emotional pain until I began to truly heal. Every physical pain I had in my body was connected to an emotional time in my life that was difficult.

The strangest thing was being able to connect to my physical pain and clear it, without having to revisit trauma... It was like a magic pill.

But wait... the best part is yet to come.

The more I practiced EFT, the more I noticed my habits, reactions, thoughts, beliefs and life all began to change. Old thoughts that I used to have, I tried to bring back but I couldn't, no matter how hard I tried. I had found my magic to change it all.

I'm now 5 years down the line since I began this 'spiritual' work and I can tell you wholeheartedly. Your mindset isn't everything: **your energy is**. Once you clear your energy, you will clear your mind, body and spirit.

Have you ever heard of Ho'oponopono?

Ho'oponopono is an ancient Hawaiian prayer that cultivates a deep level of forgiveness and release through the mind/body/spirit connection.

Dive deep into that prayer/mantra now and you'll awaken your soul's journey to stepping into this book with the love and intention for transformation that I envisioned for you.

"I'm sorry. Please forgive me. Thank you. I love you."

Repeat the above phrases seven times, whilst tapping on the collarbone — you can thank me later!

NOTE

CHAPTER 2

Getting aligned with the Law of Attraction

Oh please... let's not focus on the toxic positivity: you are allowed to have a fucking shit day. It happens. Get over yourself. If you ever hear from anyone that your emotions don't matter and you 'shouldn't feel them', tell them to fuck right off.

I can't even begin to tell you how many of my clients who have felt that at one point in their life they were told not to think negative thoughts and not to feel or honour their negative emotions, because the law of attraction says they shouldn't. This is the biggest BS I've ever heard in humankind.

We have to change this script if we want to transform and attract more of the good stuff. Law of attraction is not about ignoring what you feel, it's about honouring it and recognising what does and doesn't serve you for the highest good of all.

Every negative situation/emotion/experience/thought you have is based on you being human. Which in turn means, if you do not feel you are human or highly medicated and numb.

The human mind/body generates feeling because without them, we would be robots that don't understand what it means to love or hate. We have the five senses for a reason. Do you know what they are?

- Smell
- Taste
- See
- Feel
- Hear

These senses help us navigate life as human spirits.

You have your human spirit for a reason, and that reason is LIFE. Your heart beats, your lungs inhale and exhale… this is what we need for basic life.

When it comes to the law of attraction, if you are not feeling, you are not attracting! Keep in mind that you need to **feel** to bring abundance into your life. It's not something you can magically do with no energy ;).

Something else I often hear about the law of the attraction is: if you think it, you will have it.

Ermmmm… back up. No, it doesn't work like that either.

You must take some action to make this magic come to fruition.

The recipe I have found to catapult you to success is this:

Know, with unshakeable conviction, what you want. If you say, "I'm manifesting X amount of money into the bank" but do NOTHING to work with the universe, the money won't come. When you experience the deep inner knowing and you take action and trust that you will receive, this outcome is already yours.

Deep knowing brings confidence, trust and contentment.

You will know you are in a space of deep knowing by having a feeling of calm confidence and won't be pressuring yourself to MAKE IT HAPPEN. The force and push energy shows up as lack and scarcity; this vibration then accumulates as the opposite to what you do want.

Feel it as it's already done. Many people confuse this step with dreamy points of view. You can dream of course, no problem, but if you are dreaming and feeling the 'I WISH' vibe, then that is again bringing you to the energetic vibe of LACK.

Your vibration needs to match what you are willing to receive. It's important to take note of your vibration and either DO THE INNER work or maximise your trust and flow in the flow during the process.

Doing the inner work means you release any energy, beliefs and stories that are misaligned to your true desires. We will be repeating this message, so don't worry because I won't let you forget this bit! It's VERY IMPORTANT.

Take action to welcome it in. So many miss this part then wonder why it's not working! You do actually have to move yourself with this. Okay, let's get practical here just for a moment…

If you want something, you have to trust that your actions will bring it to fruition.

Now, let's focus on an item you want—the perfect 'for you' item that ever did exist. Do you sit there and not search the web or the shops until you find the perfect one?

The best example I can give of this is when I had decided I was buying myself a motorbike. I had no clue about the bike I wanted or how big of an engine to buy or what would be most suited to me. So, I talked about it, and talked about it with everyone. I researched it. I listened to guidance.

Then suddenly, as I was casually scrolling through the many options online, there she was. It was this beautiful pink bike that was JUST FOR ME… It only took a few days, but the universe brought it all to me… At the right place at the right time.

Another thing the universe did to guide me on this one was this: it was a Wednesday and I was childfree when I heard this voice, prompting me to message my friend and see if she was free.

I was going to suggest going to the bingo as something to do. Turned out that she was going to call me too, as it was a fun night at BINGO. That night, I was the winner of the JACKPOT and took home a tidy sum.

Trust the process. Thee mistake many people make is they don't fully believe they can have what they want, so the manifestation process gets all stagnant and stressful then they blame themselves for everything. This is why it's important to feel what is happening inside of you.

One little tip though: if you believe in yourself, you will naturally trust yourself. When you open up to the flow of trusting yourself, you will begin to naturally receive opportunities and manifest your desires.

TRUST THE PROCESS... TRUST IN YOU

Allow yourself to receive. If I had £1 for every time someone have said they are manifesting their desires, but struggle to receive, I would be a billionaire! Listen, you CAN have all you desire but your muscles that allow you to receive need stretching.

They BIG TIME need stretching.

Did you get that memo? Shall we say it again? Your ability to receive is a muscle that needs stretching.

Seriously, take a moment and think how easy it is for you to receive a compliment, a gift or a hug even? If you struggle to receive, your manifestation powers will also be a struggle to awaken.

One way for you to start stretching this receiving muscle and get playful with the universe is to connect with and love yourself for all you are and aspire to be. It's time!

Will you take the action today to love yourself a little bit more? Will you ask the universe to bring you gifts that you can openly welcome and receive with the love intended?

SOUL ALIGNED Manifesting is where the universe delivers exactly what you ask for, with ease, flow and all in the most divine timing.

TRUST THE PROCESS.

> ***EXERCISE:*** Take a moment to DREAM BIG. I Mean bigger than you have ever imagined—the billionaire lifestyle, fame, travel, love. Picture yourself in the most audacious dream lifestyle you can ever imagine.

Now tune into your feelings. How is your body reacting? What stories is your mind telling you? What beliefs are showing up for you?

Your INNER work begins here. If your body, nervous system and mind doesn't feel safe receiving all you dream of, there is work to be done.

Every single thought, feeling and belief in this moment is what will manifest your dreams into reality. Your work begins by releasing the negative BS that comes up, and doing the inner work so you can truly have all that your heart desires.

I'm going to teach you some strategies later in this book but, for now, I want to help you see the power of your mind/body connection. As I said above, what you think and feel can bring your results to reality.

I was manifesting all things good and bad... and I had no idea!

Every time I got fearful about money, I attracted debt, fines and unexpected bills. However, when I fell into trusting the process, money flew to me in abundance. Clients book discovery calls overnight and pay me in full for my 4-month packages. Unexpected opportunities drop into my inbox to collaborate and bring more clients to my world.

One podcast episode earnt me £10k... just 30 minutes of delivery led to sales amounting to 10k.

Manifesting your desires is not always easy, but you do have the power to change the vibration of what you feel to lean into, trust and manifest a new reality. Healing and overcoming all the emotions/subconscious blocks you feel will enable you to create the space of manifesting your wildest dreams.

I could talk all day about my salsa dance with the Law of Attraction. I was so deeply captivated by other people's results that I chose to learn more about it and got certified. In 2021, I became an advanced Law of Attraction Wealth Practitioner — but even then, I resisted my desires, and would avoid doing the practice for myself. I wasn't ready to receive and that's the simply truth. I wasn't ready at all.

I didn't have the self-belief, self-worth or self-compassion to see myself as worthy of having more. In my personal life and family, I was still deep in recovery and grief. Sometimes we just need to own where we are because being honest and self-aware will help you way more than you think.

There is no magic pill to resolve your manifestation nightmares. Being honest with yourself about what you really want and what you are prepared to do, to realign, overcome and adapt will enable you to have the answers you need to thrive beyond the reality of where you are right now.

The recipe to help you manifest is to feel what you want, how much you want it, the unshakeable conviction that you can have self-belief. Feel how it's going to happen and where it is showing up for you.

Take some time to sit with what you are trying to manifest, feel into your heart and be honest with yourself. Ask: is this really what I want? Or, is it what I think I want? Am I in alignment to receive what I want? Am I willing to receive?

Sit with this, let go, forgive yourself and others, raise your vibration as much as you can or ask for help. It's not a sign of weakness to feel unable to raise your vibration on your own. In fact, it's another message to the universe that you are committed to your own dreams.

Something I love about a breakthrough session is seeing the magic come alive afterwards, in both situations as coach and client. Manifestation and embodied results are one area I love to serve in.

The results always blow my mind...

- Kat went from 0 - 5 figure contracts.
- Helen was struggling to onboard clients and after one session, onboarded 3 new clients in 4 hours
- Michelle moved from lacking income expansion to quadrupling income in just a few short hours.

The magic is simply incredible. Do the work and you'll see for yourself. Check in with your vibration, and if you don't know where to start, use this journaling prompt:

"I don't know when and I don't know how, but my life is about to change because:"

Fill this in, let the pen flow and awaken your soul to what you want to manifest in your life and business; you have the power within you to create anything. Allow yourself to take the time to see what magic you want to create — the universe is listening!

NOTE

CHAPTER 3

Being Specific... Soul aligned intentions are KEY!

When was the last time you listened to your heart when making decisions? Or do you just set goals, for the sake of it?

Every day I hear from souls who are setting goals and not getting the results they truly desire: it usually means they are just setting goals for the sake of it. Doing so is not going to get you anywhere — I have the t-shirts, blood, sweat and tears to prove it!

The truth is, you have the power to create more than you ever thought possible. However, your goals need to match your energetic vibe. If dabbling in a magical pool of desires doesn't excite you, then we have some work to do!

Setting yourself a goal of 10 sales this week is just a goal. You might reach it, you might not. Is it any wonder it's not working for you?

As a spiritual entrepreneur, it's vital you follow your heart's calling. Setting clear goals, or intentions, is from the heart space, not the head space and it captivates the energy of attraction. We attract what we feel.

Okay, let's get to the nuts and bolts of intentions. When your heart is wired for the success of the matter, **nothing** will get in your way. That then creates a **Recipe for Co-Creation**.

The Art of Intention setting is wanting more than just money in the bank. It's about the bigger purpose: the people you will help, the magic you will unfold and the souls you will light up along the way.

Another way to look at intentions is: ZERO PRESSURE. Setting an intention is like making a wish and having good intentions for others, as well as yourself. You think of all the good you will do, once you have created the magic.

Now, you may be wondering who will benefit the most? I know in your heart you do what you do to help others, to serve but, more importantly, there is a legacy within you that is waiting for you to show up for.

Serving the wider community's hearts and souls will cause a ripple effect of change to come from the people you serve and that's the magic. That's the bigger picture and heartfelt intention that will move you into action.

When someone says, be specific, this is what that means... Specifically set the intentions of what you truly aim to achieve. It's not just 10 sales this week; it's 10 people you will serve, whether that be with a product or a service. Your intention runs so much deeper than just a goal.

This is your reminder to captivate that moment. To feel the bigger picture and be very specific. When your desires come from a heart space, the universe will co-create with you in magical ways.

Another way to be specific with the intentions you want to set is to also look at all the FEELS. Do you really want to have all that you are asking for? Sometimes what you want to have and what your subconscious/energetic nervous system says are two entirely different things altogether, as per the last chapter. What you feel and what you want must be an energetic match.

Here's another **exercise** for you to test if you are in alignment with your specific request:

Stand up and place your hands by the side of your body. Stand still. Ask your body to communicate with you. Ask your body to move on the vibration of 'yes'. It will either move you forwards or backwards.

Then ask your body to move on the vibration of 'no'. It will again either move forward or backwards.

If what you want is a match, your body will respond with a yes, and if it's not a vibrational match, it will say no. Your body talks to you every day, so listen to it.

Many of my clients come to me with an idea/vision/dream/desire, but it's not working for them. It leads to all kinds of stress and frustrations, which negatively impacts their self-esteem. This happens when the subconscious is blocking you from finding your true calling / purpose. Your subconscious wants you to be safe, so when you are in this predicament, the healing work/inner work is where you need to begin.

As you progress through this book, you will see the pattern here; the energetic vibe and your soul's calling is not always as clear as it seems. The energetic shift is what will bring you back to having all desire in life and business.

SOUL ALIGNMENT is a real thing! Intentionally creating soul alignment is magic, and a fast way to create magnetic abundant success, YOUR WAY.

Crafting a business you love **MUST** be the most potent part of your business development. Why? Because it's you who must put this into action. I've seen it time and time again, where entrepreneurs are struggling to build their businesses. Nine times out of ten, it's due to the misaligned guidance and perceptions they have around 'what business should be' after they have listened to all the online noise. They take on everybody's opinion and then get themselves stuck in an overwhelmed state, doing all the 'busy' stuff that are not cash generating activities.

YAWN... I'm bored of it now. I'm here for the trailblazers, the rebel makers and the mavericks who consciously choose to do things their own way.

YOU are reading this book because your soul knows you are meant for more.

THE SOUL ALIGNED WAY...

Okay, I know you are probably thinking, what does this really mean though Vicki? It means you must reclaim your power. You say no more to the BS in the online space, and finally listen to your soul's wisdom of what you can and will achieve.

Are you with me on this journey to create a world where spiritual entrepreneurs no longer hide their magic and use their inner powers to create success beyond their wildest dreams?

I'm hoping you said yes and are going to continue reading because I promise you, this information will help change your life and business for good.

Remember, it's not enough to just say you want success, you must absolutely mean it. Wholeheartedly MEAN IT.

Place your hands over your heart space now and let's do a self-declaration:

"I (insert name) solemnly declare that I am on this journey to create a bigger impact, to serve others but, more importantly, to love what I do and step into a life of creating abundant happiness."

As I type this chapter to you, I want you to know something important. Your happiness is more important than anything else. Being happy doing what you want to do, being in your zone of genius is the most important thing of all.

Let's take a moment to reflect on some global icons and their success.

Robin Williams was a creator of comedy and loved globally, yet he battled his whole life with depression. A more recent departure on this earth plane was Matthew Perry, a gentleman loved globally for his kindness, wit and charm, spent his life battling addictions, whilst serving others.

With all the fame and fortune in the world, two of the most heart-centred souls carried on fighting battles behind the scenes that most people weren't aware of. They were here to serve the world while being two of the most unhappy souls on the planet.

These are just two examples of thousands of famous icons. Whitney Houston, Elvis, Johnny Cash, Amy Winehouse and

Judy Garland, are few more. I don't want the same result for you.

My wish for you is that you bring into this business of yours an opportunity to fill your heart with the most amazing unconditional love for yourself AND others. So, whether you are just starting out or a seasoned entrepreneur... It's time to really listen to your heart's song and change any part of your business that is not lighting you up, not serving your mission and not supporting YOUR HAPPINESS first.

Your soul aligned intentions will carve a path for you that brings you the most joy, so that your working life and home

life are the most magical of all. Bringing your dreams to reality is what this book will help you to achieve as it's a personal journey for business expansion.

Soul aligned success is the most beautiful way to cultivate your own dreams and the dreams of others. It starts with soul alignment and soul aligned intentions. NOT GOALS.

Feel into your heart and create the intentions that will light you up to change the world as we know it.

NOTE

CHAPTER 4

Getting Clarity: Who, What, Where and When

So far in this book, we have covered mindset, energy, law of attraction and intentions... but now it's time to shift into more clearer business development guidance to help you rocket launch your business into the stratosphere of magical abundance.

Inside my signature programme, The Fast Track Business Accelerator, module 1 is my favourite. It's the real eye opener to help you cultivate soul alignment in your business for abundant success and help you grow towards your 6-figure empire. Why am I telling you this? Because in this chapter, I'm going to share a sneak peek of that programme with you, to help you cultivate your soul aligned business for growth and expansion.

To help you set soul aligned intentions for your business as a spiritual entrepreneur, you need to cultivate the truth of what you really want and WHO you deeply want to serve.

Imagine 6 months from now, you've unlocked all the magic you had inside, your business has expanded and you know exactly who you are serving. As a result, ou are lighting up the world with your magic, you are recognised for all that you bring to the world, you feel so happy and content in your own skin, you are trying new things, achieving new intentions and more importantly, bringing your bigger vision dreams into reality.

Or for the more seasoned entrepreneur; you ditched the struggle bus, got soul aligned, had clarity over your messaging and turned over 5-6 figures in your business every single month.

All of this is possible in your business.

It's your time now to believe it, feel it and achieve it. Let's get to work.

Inside your business right now, you will have a service or product that you want to sell to the world. Offering this service is where we are going to start to help you elevate your business today!

Let's get a checklist going here:

- ✓ You love your offer of 110% and know it's going to have global impact.

- ✓ The pricing of your offer is so damn good you don't mind hearing no for those who are not ready for it — you KNOW the magic this offer provides.
- ✓ You talk about your offer every single day.
- ✓ Your audience is hot AF, they love you and can't wait for you to show up and deliver.
- ✓ Your offer sells with ease and flow.
- ✓ Your systems are automated it feels magical.
- ✓ Your work life balance is in order and flows.
- ✓ Cash flows with ease and abundantly every single day.
- ✓ You have fun consistently in your life and business.
- ✓ You are creative and in your flow, CONSISTENTLY.
- ✓ Waking up every day is a pleasure.
- ✓ You have time and freedom to live your life, your way

Okay, so how many of these do you tick so far?

Let's face it... 11/11 is hard to grasp. Entrepreneurs with a spiritual mind often have way more ebbs and flows in their business due to the creativity that flows and the new ideas that land. New projects and changes that come with new levels.

Let's iron out the BS beliefs that you need all 11/11 ticked to have the perfectly aligned business, because that doesn't exist. Being in business means there will be times that are busier than others, you will have an array of projects, collaborations and growth spurts with comedowns! The checklist above is a guide for you to see what is working so far and what isn't.

Two of the above points are a really great way to predict where business is heading.

Audience and Sales.

Example:

Your audience is flat and not engaged = sales are limited

Audience building is by far your greatest income generating activity... and this is usually the first hurdle to climb when launching a new offer, product or service. If you don't have a hot audience, you won't have success. This is a very harsh but true reality.

Let's figure out who your audience really is.

Now, please don't be fooled by all those on INSTA with 50K audiences as most of the people that follow are misaligned and not actively buying their offers. I've sat with multi-millionaires with audiences of over 200K struggling to get tangible results for their projects to fly. What were they missing? The right audience...

There are a few key things to consider when thinking about this: Who is in your ideal audience? Do you know who they are? Do you know how they feel? Do you understand what they need?

Niching down can feel like a never-ending cycle of BS... constantly thinking about their needs, wants and desires, how you can best serve or help them. Most people hate niching down, as this cultivates a restriction and feelings of fear that you are leaving people out.

Let me share this little secret with you:

"Your soul and heart know who you are here to serve, and it's time to listen to that calling."

Instead of cultivating a 'I HAVE TO' attitude, let's create a 'I am ready to, attitude'.

Who are you READY to serve at this point in your business? Listen into your heart space and figure out who is this SOUL you are ready to serve. We are not talking cars / houses / jobs; we are talking about soul connections.

Suddenly, everything starts to 'fit'. You no longer struggle to reach those who need you, your messaging and heart are all in the right place at the right time. The universe begins to work with you in co-creating the magic of connection. You then begin to start attracting full paying clients out of nowhere! Literally.

Do you have a soul connection with those you are serving already? If you do, you will know what I mean. Or maybe you are reading this and just needing a reminder that you can go back to soul connections to reach those you are ready to serve.

Remember, the heart knows way more than the mind, so listen to it and trust the process.

Getting clarity on who your soul aligned clients / customers are will change your life and business. I often hear 'business-minded gurus' say things like, business isn't emotional, so don't make it emotional and all will be good.

YUCK. That energy stinks.

As a spiritual entrepreneur, you will also feel the same repulsion and know that this vibe is not for you. Those who are successful with a non-emotional drive, do have a centered approach, even if they don't believe it! You'll see it in them.

PAY ATTENTION: YOU ARE NOT HERE TO FIT INTO THEIR BOX. Let's do you boo!

Now, the nitty gritty details you'll hear every business strategist, marketing consultant and business coach on the planet say:

WHO IS YOUR IDEAL CLIENT?

What you have hopefully taken away by now is the need to avoid fitting into a box. We are not creating an avatar of a person. As a spiritual entrepreneur, you are gaining clarity of the souls you are ready to serve.

Dreamy AF Clients are heading your way as soon as you open your heart to those soul aligned intentions of:

- Who you will serve
- Why you will serve them

- What they need from you
- What you will help them with
- How it feels to work with them
- How they feel working with you
- The client / customer relationship you will have
- The ripple effect of your work together
- The overall outcome of that energy exchange
- What will they say after working together
- What does the monetary exchange feel like?
- Is it a soul aligned dreamy experience for you both?

Feel free to use these points as journaling prompts to help you CALL in your ideal soul aligned clients. The deeper you go with this, the stronger your message will be in your marketing, social media, networking and, more importantly, in your heart.

When you are soul aligned to WHO, the rest works itself out.

My role in the Fast Track Business Accelerator Programme is to help you become soul aligned to your business, so you can finally attract your soul aligned clients / customers who will stay with you for years to come.

Your role now is to use this chapter to captivate / revisit your SOUL ALIGNED DREAMY AF clients, take some time, burn some sage then get yourself in a quiet, relaxed and mindful state. That way, you can shine and bring the magic of your heart to the hearts of thousands more souls who are actively waiting for you to level TF up.

The Soul Aligned Offer for multiple 5-figure months and a 6-figure empire.

Now you've taken time to figure out your soul aligned clients, or at least have an idea of who your heart wants you to serve, let's elevate your offerings, services and products.

Creating a soul aligned offer to reach the hearts of your soul connected clients brings you to magnetic vibes of co-creation with the universe, collapsing time, releasing resistance and flowing with peaceful gains.

Many people don't understand the true meaning of soul alignment. I have mentioned it quite a lot so far inside this book, so I am particularly hopeful that you know what I mean by now.

Are you now ready to captivate the hearts of your soul aligned clients and bring them something they are going to bite your hand off for? Metaphorically speaking of course.

Inside of you is this magical idea that is not currently out there serving in the way you had hoped. Perhaps there's a little tweak you can make. Now that you've reflected on your dreamy AF client awareness, I'm sure you can begin to feel the misaligned energy that was, and the new level high vibe ideas will start to roll on in.

If you are not flowing magical ways to elevate your offers / packages / bundles/ products for 5-figure months and beyond, let's take a moment to dive in.

Inside my FREE Soul aligned 5 figure offers PDF, we have some really magical journaling prompts. Here's are a few extra to get you started:

1. What does your dreamy AF ideal client need?
2. If they could wave a magic wand and fix ONE thing, what would that be?
3. What makes your offer better than anything else out there on the market?
4. What would your dreamy clients want differently to what you have on offer now?
5. What don't you want to offer anymore?
6. Is the pricing still where it needs to be for your skills, expertise, time and experience?
7. What is a number 1 non-negotiable for your upleveled dreamy AF client? How will you implement that?

Need help with all these questions? I hear ya! It's not easy diving in and trying to figure it all out, so don't!

Step 1: Visit the link or scan the code below

https://vickichisholm.com/soulaligned5figureoffer/

To grab your FREE PDF and Masterclass

Step 2: Get yourself into a relaxed state and be curious about what could flow from your soul to that pen on a piece of paper. Allow your mind to explore the infinite possibilities of creating magic and awakening next level abundance.

Abundance, in this instance, means time freedom and fabulous clients to work with… <u>on demand</u>.

Let's get to work!

NOTE

CHAPTER 5

Your Money Mindset, Pricing and Overcoming Blocks

The most valuable piece of work you could ever do is working on your money mindset… Even multimillionaires and billionaires must consistently work on their money mindset. It's a way of life when you weren't born with a millionaire lifestyle. Even though some people have been born into the millions, it doesn't mean they have a healthy relationship with money, so it is vital that they work on their mindset. Money mindset is quite taboo for spiritual entrepreneurs, and this is one element of the work I do that I know will be a catalyst for change for years to come.

I am talking levelling the fuck up with what you allow yourself to receive.

Who would you be if you allowed yourself to be the catalyst for change in your life? One thing I've learnt with my journey and my clients is this:

With money comes a whole host of baggage!

It really captivates my mind to see that the energy of money can cause so much fear, uncertainty and misery for so many, yet it's just energy. It honestly mind-boggles me. When I learnt about money being an energy, I soon came to establish what my relationship with money was... and what an eye opener that was. I had this belief:

Money = Love

But it went deeper than just that statement...

Love = Abuse

This was my relationship with money, so as you can imagine, I didn't want it. If money = love and love = abuse in my mind's eye, then why on earth would I want money?

Of course, none of this was a conscious thing: this was hidden deep down in my subconscious and playing out in my life! It sucked; it was awful to experience, especially as a mother!

When I first started out in business in 2012, I was a Virtual Assistant, ready to help with all those admin needs. I was a qualified bookkeeper, tech savvy and a, social media whizz, yet I only charged £10ph. Getting new clients became the hardest challenge I had ever faced in my entire life.

I had no clue about business, and I was used to being paid in exchange for a paid role....

Now, let's backtrack to when I was 18 and earning a small fortune every single month after busting my ass for 60-80 hours a week! I earnt every damn penny of that income. I was classed as a workaholic.

Working hard and receiving money wasn't an issue for me, but then, as I progressed with this business, I had no idea what I was doing. Onboarding clients felt like walking through tar and getting blood from a stone.

Don't get me wrong, clients came in, but it wasn't enough to pay the bills… It was hard as fuck and all my children were under the age of 8 at the time. I was living through domestic abuse, unaware of what I was really experiencing and broke. Flat broke. It crushed my soul… for the first time in my adult life, I couldn't provide for my family.

My body was breaking down. I had fibromyalgia, chronic fatigue, severe anxiety, depression, minimal support, house to upkeep, food to put on the table and 3 children to look after. Some people would argue that I was in a relationship… but those who understand the situation know I wasn't in a loving, supportive relationship. I was ALONE.

It's not easy to look back at or discuss this part of my life, but I wanted to share the raw realness that I have experienced, so you can find the courage to overcome any shame you may have about your journey too. I was ashamed, lost and confused. Thankfully, it didn't last too long, and the money started slowly coming in… very very slowly.

Once I discovered the law of attraction, I decided to level up my game. I know it's me who creates my reality. I can choose fear or I can choose to reclaim my power and overcome all I was led to believe.

It wasn't that easy though... When it came to changing my life, I did that in 2015. I said no more, walked away and after 5 months of being 'homeless' with my children, we were staying with family and friends, until I could resettle. In the end, I accepted a council property as I wasn't able to pay for private rental, nor was I in the position to buy somewhere.

My journey continued and my story didn't change much. I had knowledge and awareness, but nothing was really changing.

Fast forward another year, my healing journey quickly took a turn for the worst and I was suddenly burnt out and battling a disease at age 30. My business was growing and had just turned over 6 figures ... not bad from just £10ph at the start, eh? But I couldn't sustain working those long hours. I didn't NEED MY JOB to cope with life anymore. I let go of EVERYTHING.

I later discovered I had com plex PTSD from years of emotional, mental, financial and sexual abuse. I was having to scrape my ass off the floor every single day to be able to be a mum. The outside world saw me functioning, but my inside world was the lowest it had ever been.

Something had to change.

When you reach the gutter, this is often when you decide to make the biggest turnarounds in your life. I am no stranger to the gutter and what took me years to discover was this is a very normal human experience. Go figure! I thought I was an outcast because I didn't fit in. I was having these horrific experiences while feeling worthless, alone and ashamed. Yet everything I had gone through, millions of others had too! It was a sad but eye opening fact. There is no shame when you see life-changing opportunities happen, and you fully surrender to it being circumstance and not a definition of who you are.

Remember my old belief: money = love, love = abuse. It is beliefs like this that feeds the story of your experience.

Shame is not REAL... it's a perception. Shame is only brought on by how you judge yourself and how you allow others' judgments to affect you. Shame is not here to control you; shame is an energy that is not even yours. It's something you've adopted about how you SHOULD feel given that you may have behaved wrongly.

Shame is for those moments where vindictiveness, callousness, jealousy, rage, murder, revenge and unnecessary behaviours are acted out. Money shame is not real. It's just energy.

Your money story is what will change your life. When you become aware of the story you hold within, you can decide to change it. Majority of my clients come to me with one thing in mind: BUSINESS INCOME.

However, the business income is only a by-product of how you view money and what it means to you. Many coaches out there will tell you to do business with zero emotion attached to it, but for you, as a spiritual entrepreneur, that approach won't work. Which means you have work to do!

So now I have given you some insights into the money mind set / energy stories I was holding, I would love you to stay with me as I work through the energy of pricing.

Pricing your services is only a starting point of your business growth and getting this bit 'right' can feel like hell on earth if your money mindset is in the gutter, filled with shame, fear and disempowering stories of yucky, worthless hell.

Let's do some EFT on this... If you have never tried tapping, (Emotional Freedom Technique - an energy psychology modality, using Chinese acupressure to stimulate the meridian points on the body to move energy and bring your body back into balance) then let me tell you this! It changed my life.

Energy Psychology rewires your brain and shifts stagnant energy from the mind, body and soul. As we have spoken of shame, I welcome you to take a moment to feel into your body where you are holding the energy of shame. On a scale of 0-10, how intense is this energy that has shown up for you?

The SUDs - Subjective Units of Distress are used with 10+ being intense and 0 being no reaction at all.

Make a note of how you feel and the intensity.

It's simple and easy to follow. Take full responsibility for yourself and give this a try.

Using the image guide overleaf taken from my Tapping out the Blocks PDF Guide (see back of book for resources.)

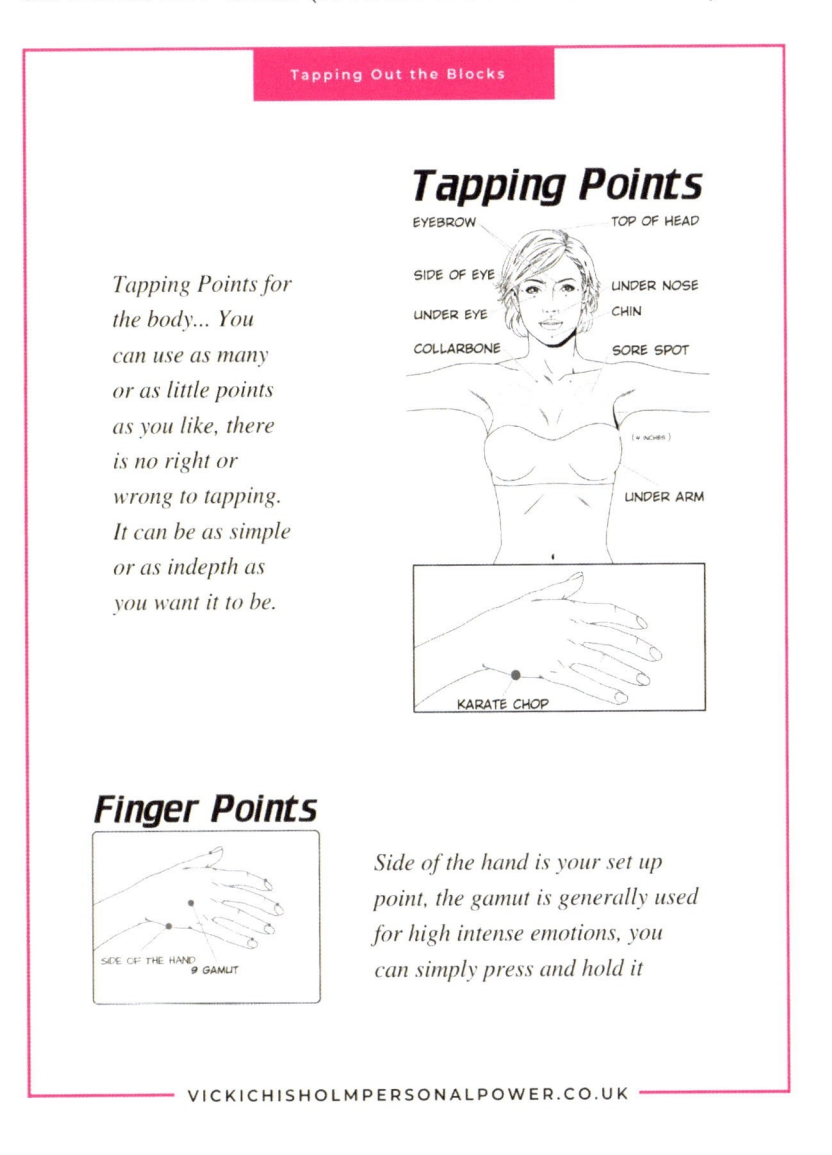

Tapping Out the Blocks

Tapping Points

- EYEBROW
- SIDE OF EYE
- UNDER EYE
- COLLARBONE
- TOP OF HEAD
- UNDER NOSE
- CHIN
- SORE SPOT
- (4 INCHES)
- UNDER ARM
- KARATE CHOP

Tapping Points for the body... You can use as many or as little points as you like, there is no right or wrong to tapping. It can be as simple or as indepth as you want it to be.

Finger Points

SIDE OF THE HAND
9 GAMUT

Side of the hand is your set up point, the gamut is generally used for high intense emotions, you can simply press and hold it

VICKICHISHOLMPERSONALPOWER.CO.UK

Tapping on the side of your hand - between your little finger and wrist and repeat:

"Even though I have all this money shame and fear in my body, I choose to deeply and completely love and accept myself."

Repeat this on the side of the hand x 3 while focusing on your breath and staying present.

Then move on to the other meridian points on the body, tapping on the following points and repeating:

Eyebrow: This money shame

Side of the eye: The energy of money shame

Under the eye: This money shame in my body

Under the nose: All this energy around money shame

Chin: All this energy of shame

Collarbone: I choose to see it for what it is

Under the arm: this energy of shame

Top of the head: It's safe for me to release this energy now

Repeat the above exercise until you feel a shift inside your body. If the energy hasn't shifted, repeat until it does. You will need to drink plenty of water after this exercise.

(If you would like some help, feel free to reach out. All details are on the back of this book for 1:1 breakthrough sessions and my powerful AF 28 days to personal power self-help programme.)

Okay, now you've done this exercise, you'll be able to connect with how it feels inside. Now, ba k to pricing.

Of course there is always a method to my madness; I felt it would be appropriate to clear any stagnant energy now, so we can enter the world of pricing for you to be true to yourself and awaken your worth!

With shame now dissipated or at least reduced, let's talk aligned pricing vs strategic pricing.

Aligned pricing VS Strategic pricing and how they come together

How do you price your current offerings, do you feel into your heart space or do you look at the market research and throw a magic number at it then pray for the best?

No judgment, you are doing what felt / feels good to you, in that moment. But can I please suggest we change that now. Ultimately, pricing your offer, service or product will needt to be in alignment with your values, worth and inner confidence of your delivery to sell.

If you are not in alignment and your pricing makes you feel underpaid, undervalued, underappreciated or too far out of reach, I can assure you that selling at that price will be like going to the dentist and asking them to pull your teeth out just for fun!

Perhaps you can already relate to that?!

We know what it feels like to not be in alignment, so let's shift and move your offerings into pricing alignment. We'll break it down into two sections:

Aligned Pricing - When you are in alignment with your offer and pricing, this is when you will feel confident as fuck showing up and talking about the money exchange. Notice my language here. MONEY EXCHANGE.

Aligned pricing takes you to a space in your heart, where you know the value of the service / product / offer you are delivering, and you will not waiver on this. You will lovingly release those who do not see your worth and wish them well on their journey. You no longer feel afraid to not meet other people's needs and you will hold firm in your boundaries with calm confidence. You will also welcome those who are ready to pay in full and you won't be holding silent parties inside - as this is your new normal.

Aligned pricing brings you peace, joy, connection and wealth.

Strategic pricing hits the nail on the head, as it pleases your business coach, and serves to bring in an income you desire. For example:

- 10 × £100 = £1000
- 5 × £2500 = £12.5K
- 3 × £10k = £30k

Strategy allows you to see how you will piece those numbers together to reach financial goals and incentives. Plus, it gives your accountant a cash flow projection, and your business coach a clear indication of what needs to be done to reach targets. All of which is a positive in the tick box of to do's if you choose to follow a structured process.

Strategy also allows you to see what will 'work' and what won't. Whilst strategy is important, so is alignment, which is why I choose, as a business development coach and strategist, to teach you both aspects of the pricing structure for elevated success. Alignment and abundance go hand in hand, but the numbers in business DO matter if you want financial freedom.

When you combine aligned pricing with strategic pricing, your heart becomes full and your business expands daily.

Now for the juicy bit!

How to create an aligned pricing strategy that gives you the financial and emotional freedom to easily exchange your service/offer/product for money? Here's how: answer these questions and **DO THE INNER WORK!**

1. What is my dreamy AF income desire? Feel into this whole heartedly and allow yourself to dream bigger than ever before.
2. Why can't I have that? Make a list, go deeper than you've ever gone and clear any residing BS from your energetic field.

3. Why am I deserving of this income and business success?
4. What will my life look like when I am serving and receiving on this level?
5. Does my offer align with the value I want to charge? Feel into this
6. Will my ideal dreamy as fuck client be ready to pay me in full? What objections might I face?
7. Will this pricing structure support me towards my goals?
8. Is it safe for me to have this level of financial success?
9. Why can't I overcome my barriers to have my desires?
10. Who am I as this soul aligned, financially wealthy business owner?

Of course you can add to these questions, you can meditate, journal or EFT your way through. It doesn't matter HOW you do this work, all that matters is that you do.

Don't be afraid to flow with intuitive nudges to fully listen to the inner fears of doubts or insecurities. Listen with love, listen without judgment, trust yourself to navigate this journey to help you serve the world.

You've got this and I'm here holding your hand to get this DONE.

NOTE

CHAPTER 6

Understanding soul wounds & how they impact your business life and sabotage your dreams!

A slightly off-track topic, but this is a deep one that most people ignore and then beat themselves up. They can't figure out why they are still lost in the transition of pain, despite walking, climbing and moving what feels like ten trips up and over Mount Kilimanjaro.

One of the main contributors towards burn out is pushing through when, logically, all seems as it 'should' and all 'should' work as it is intended. But then you find yourself having to work harder, and harder without zero results.

One of the best statements my mentor ever gave me was this:

> *"Should, 'should' be banned - it's a reflection of judgment and lack of self-trust."*

Then the internal questions start:

- ❖ "Why can't I move through this?"
- ❖ "Why am I so stuck?"
- ❖ "Why can't I change this story?"
- ❖ "Why am I still replaying these stories?"

Most people will look at the strategy, themselves or even external sources and enter the BLAME CULTURE… this then feeds into all the areas that aren't even to blame for the reality of what is really happening.

The element of blame that comes forward is the natural state of the human mind, but you are a spiritual entrepreneur, not here to just live in the human mind.

Remember your truth here and your soul connection to the heart centred truth you were born with.

It's time to remember your soul's journey and go explore with your journal in hand if needs be. Your 3d reality reflects your soul's story. Yet logic, strategy, coaches, healers and mentors are the ones that are blamed for things not working.

A word here that may come as a bit of a trigger is Responsibility. Even deeper than that, is radical **SELF**-responsibility.

Hold up though… It goes even deeper than that. Your soul's self-responsibility is to remember why you are struggling with this, and to awaken those triggers so you can overcome those hurdles. This is where you get to be the catalyst of change in all areas magical and transformational. Dig deep my friend; it's time to rocket launch your soul into success.

Every single time you feel 'stuck', 'resistant', 'unheard', 'afraid', 'unsure', 'angry', you are triggering something in your soul's story.

Take a look at one area in your business right now that might not be working, such as marketing, sales, content, expansion, visibility, connection, relationships, etc.... one area might be causing you sleepless nights, chronic anxiety and heart palpitations. There is generally a reason why this is happening and the surface level is where this problem is rising from.

The REAL issue is usually hidden in your soul's subconscious.

Good news though as you get to tap into that magic to find the answers you are looking for. Before I get you to do this work on your own, let me share some key indicators of what you might be looking for.

My personal journey with soul wounds:

> I found life overwhelming, stressful and like a constant battle. Every single corner I turned was another mountain, energetic block, and story of struggle to be had. I was resistant to being seen. I didn't want my voice heard. It wasn't safe for me to receive large sums of money; in fact, it wasn't safe for me to have money at all.

SKINT> BROKE> ALONE > MISUNDERSTOOD = FAILURE

Deep-rooted, worthless, pathetic, failure.

- I didn't understand why.
- I lived in struggle.
- I lived in fear of scarcity and lack.
- I had no idea why these stories were on repeat.
- I also had no idea how to break the cycles.

At the age of 18 years old, I was earning a decent wage, but always broke.

I single-handedly provided for others whilst working 60-80 hours a week. Money never seemed to be something I had but later in my journey, I discovered a phrase called financial abuse. That was one story that my 18-year-old self didn't realise she was experiencing. As I began unpacking lots of these stories about my repeating patterns from this lifetime, and childhood, I was healing, releasing and overcoming then I would be back in the same story! The frustration, the burnout, the resistance and disempowering beliefs were getting stronger and stronger. I was becoming worn out with my healing journey.

Until one day, I realised my soul's story runs deeper than just this lifetime. My soul's story goes all the way back through centuries. It all became clearer as I began to familiarise myself with old soul wounds and the plot thickened.

Let's go back to my mid-twenties, when I had always wanted to explore more spiritual things, such as self-healing tools. I was SOOO pulled to Reiki, tarot, mediumship, spirits afterlife, but I was also terrified of the unknown. I used to say to myself, how wonderful it would be to use my hands to heal others. I would imagine playing with spells and the magic that we could create. I lived in a world of imagination and daydreaming an easier life. Yet in this lifetime, my 3d reality would shut it all down and take it all out of context.

Then it all clicked, and my subconscious was communicating with me, not that I was aware at the time. I found myself saying: "I've been cursed", "I must have been a witch in a former life". Fast forward to 2017... I was now in my 31st year on the planet and I had the vision/memory and the story unfolded. NO WONDER I WAS STUCK.

My subconscious took me back to a time in the 1800s when I was a healer — AKA witch — and the only way to survive was to keep quiet, heal without the word spreading and not be in the limelight.

I was holding several witch wounds as a healer in those times I was classed as a witch. What an insight it was to see why I loved the woo woo so much. But wait... the emotional scar ring I had experienced in that lifetime is what was keeping me stuck in this lifetime.

> I was afraid of being seen - marketing wasn't safe.
>
> I was afraid of being heard - my message and voice needed to be hidden.

I was afraid of standing out - staying in poverty was safer.

I was afraid of the responsibility from others' blame - it wasn't safe.

My powers were seen as witchcraft - my healing abilities were belittled.

My soul's wounds were so real, that my soul was replaying these stories.

The hardest part of this journey was that my soul had chosen a life of more abuse / trauma, as it was safer than to be seen as the magical manifester and gifted healer I had the skills to create.

It took me 29 years to wake the fuck up and start changing those patterns. It took me 37 years to own my magic, love my innate power and reclaim my soul's journey as a psychic healer and transformation specialist.

How many years has it taken you to get to this part so far?

Perhaps you are on the journey and loving the transformations you experience. Perhaps you are only just starting. Either way, let's not use this as another BS excuse to beat yourself up with. Take this time to give yourself permission to set an intention to be free. Revisit chapters 2,3 & 4 if you want to set new intentions and get clarity.

However, we are here right now and I promised to get you started with some magically intuitive soul wound discovery.

It's your turn now to establish your soul wounds and how they are impacting your business as a spiritual entrepreneur.

Exercise

Step 1: Take some deep breaths, focus on heart centre, place your hands where you feel they need to go i.e.: chakras or lap and sit in silence for 30-60 seconds, setting the intention to your subconscious to communicate truth with you.

Step 2: Ask some key questions:

a) Do I have unhealed soul wounds causing me issues in my business?
b) What is this soul wound trying to protect me from?
c) Am I ready to heal this wound?
d) What could I achieve once I release this wound?
e) Who am I without this wound?
f) What impact will be releasing this wound have on myself and others?
g) Can I find compassion for myself and this journey whilst I am releasing this wound?

As you ask / answer these questions, it's important to follow your soul's intuition, and connect with your aligned healing tools. Earlier in this book, I shared a quick tool such as EFT. Here's a recap for how you can use this for soul wounds:

Tapping on the side of the hand and enter into a set up phrase:

Repeat x 3: "Even though I have these soul wounds that I may not have been aware of in the past, I choose to deeply and completely love and accept myself as I move through this process"

> **Eyebrow:** These soul wounds
>
> **Side of Eye:** I am aware they exist
>
> **Under the eye:** It's safe for me to acknowledge these stories now
>
> **Under the Nose**: I'm open to releasing these stories from my energetic being
>
> **Chin:** It's safe now to change the story
>
> **Collarbone:** I acknowledge my truth and detach from this being my reality
>
> **Under the arm**: I'm open to healing now

Repeat the above until your emotions are calm and then play around with what you feel drawn to say / tap on.

If tapping is not for you, I totally understand, so please don't feel obligated to follow a suggestion I make. I simply share the tools that have changed my life but you must find what works for you.

Other tools you can use:

- Energetic chord cutting
- Meditation
- Past life regression
- Angelic / 9th Dimensional realm clearing

- Timeline therapy
- Journaling
- Karma clearing, and so forth

Remember you don't have to do this alone; I recommend you work with a professional if you have strong emotional reactions to this chapter. It should be someone who can hold space for you, and guide you with love and safety: someone you trust and can work well with.

(Of course, I offer Radically Aligned Breakthrough Sessions too if my work aligns with you. Visit: www.vickichisholm.com for more)

Layering is a part of the process of healing. As soon as you heal one layer, another one comes up. The good side of this journey is this the deeper you go, the more magical your business, life, relationships and abundance become. Remember you picked up this book with a focus on becoming magnetic to abundant success. The magic lies in the depth you are willing to go within your soul.

Before I wrap up this chapter, let me take you down the exposed path of misguided self-love. Some real-life stories of misguided self-love and self-sabotage. I believe knowing and recognising these traits is vital for your expansive growth as a spiritual entrepreneur. Plus, I want to help you overcome these mistakes I see others make on a regular basis.

Past life / Karmic / Soul healing is one aspect of the journey that is often overlooked in the 3d way of living. However, the dangerous part of the journey is the self-sabotage from the subconscious and how it prevents you from getting to the root. It is for this reason that I recommend working with someone who specialises in this work.

Your subconscious knows how to keep you stuck in loops; it changes the story and ultimately the trajectory of what you are trying to achieve. It acts out of misguided self-love.

Being aware of this is a game changer.

Imagine you are just getting to the root of the issue and suddenly you need to pee, eat, check social media, text someone or do something away from the task you are supposed to be doing. It takes you to a different story or/ tells you to check your phone: anything to keep you apart from what you are about to achieve.

GOT YA. In that moment, your subconscious has veered you away from the root cause of the issue and prevented you from reaching success.

The subconscious won.

You are not given permission to go there. So, the cycle, pattern and story you don't want to play out anymore continues and this is how procrastination is born. Mis guided self-love. Pay attention! Where else are you misguided with stories of misguided self-love?

NOTE

CHAPTER 7

Your Inner Rebel Marketing

Get SEEN, HEARD AND HIRED!

Yes, I'm talking to you. There isn't anyone else reading this with you, is there?! Careful, that could be a trick question!

Okay, all joking aside, you need a decent marketing plan if you want to attract your ideal client and step into the magic of the world you are creating for yourself, your family and all those amazing souls you want to help along the way.

A quick recap. So far in this book, we have covered mindset, energy, law of attraction, getting clarity on what you want in your business/life, money, pricing and soul wounds. The next step forward is to move the needle a little deeper and awaken your soul to being heard, and seen. That means it's time to cultivate your soul aligned messaging and make sure it pops, bangs and screams "hell yeah" to your ideal client / customer, in a way that feels good to you. I absolutely fucking rock at helping my clients do this but, for myself, I SUCK! Not literally of course but I just don't have the natural flair for standing out. My 'natural way of being' is to soften things, come from a place of love and compassion. So, to step into my authoritative voice and be opinionated through content has certainly taken me some time to learn. Why am I telling you this? Because 90% of my clients have a similar issue. They are great at being everyone else's voice / cheerleader but struggle to toot their own horn.

Ultimately, as a spiritual entrepreneur, you may find this bit the hardest of all, as the subconscious wounds we worked through in the last chapter may cause you to feel very uncomfortable when speaking up and being seen. Awareness will help you overcome that though. Remember to be a witness of those thoughts rather than internalising them. Journal if you need to.

Fear of judgment and persecution are two of the biggest wounds you may discover when working to get clear on your marketing and visibility mission. Overcoming that, we can act now to help you embody the safety and stabilisation to be seen, heard and ultimately hired. Your mind could be living out of sync with your current 3d reality, so this is your nudge to shift that and cultivate a new way of being, for your highest good of all. Remember you are doing this to serve others, as well as achieve your dreams.

"It's a double impact jammy whammy kick ass movement. So, let's get it aligned first!"

Okay… Here goes: Your message is the magic sauce.

Did you hear that? **The magic you can create is in the MESSAGE.**

One thing about marketing that nobody tells you is to make it simple for yourself. Find your KEY message and then create 1000 ways to share that message. This really is the golden nugget wisdom of marketing. It is honing in on what you are truly doing.

What's your main message, calling, mission, passion and / or purpose?

Your main message is what you share through marketing that enables you to have visibility and talks to the soul of your dreamy clients.

Yet this is one area that most entrepreneurs struggle with. Give me someone else's marketing and I'm there with bells on, crafting their message and honing in on their skills. But me and my own… DAMN, it's been tough! It's been sooo tough I don't even know where to begin to tell you how I struggled with my own…

Another story that the 'Gurus' won't share is that your marketing can be super simple and the reason you are struggling with it is because of how you feel about yourself inside.

It's totally an inside job… if you didn't have resistance to it, you would just do it. So how you feel / think is a major part of your business development.

One of the ways I managed to share my message was by putting myself in CLIENT mode, and pretending I was writing content for a client in my field who needed to share my message. It worked temporarily, then I discovered I needed more authenticity in what I was doing because people can pick up on your lack of authenticity. I know it may sound crazy, but I can literally sense how someone is feeling through their words… It's a vibe and it is felt deeply, sharply and intensely. ESPECIALLY with highly sensitive, intuitive people and empaths… They just 'know!'

Another trick to add to your toolbox is that deep 'knowing' from your intuitive gifts.I Instead of looking outside of yourself and asking for feedback, ask your inner wisdom, "Is this message right for me?" The answer will be no, yes or almost. You will feel it in some way.

If you are clairsentient or claircognizant, you will be able to tap into your own inner guidance, which will give you the 'knowing' you are looking for. But honestly, you have to learn to trust your instincts and stop seeking external validation. This goes for everyone… It's not just a woo woo thing… Self-trust and learning to be your own mentor is a true skill to master, but it will give you the power to reclaim your success and own it.

This is how the mind causes conflict and pain sometimes… I literally sent some work to my coach and asked for her

Feedback but, truth is, it wasn't her feedback I needed. It was my own. It was like being a child and asking if my colouring, despite it being all outside the lines, was good enough. Honestly, it really caught me offguard when I reflected… The inner child shows up in lots of different ways: so do subconscious blocks, resistance and limiting beliefs.

I had to give myself a serious talking too before I ask for anyone else's feedback. Tuning in and asking myself what I think first is the time saving tool to generate the success.

This is something to consider embodying, especially for your Marketing Message. Are you ready to get clear on what that is and how you can share that message?

I hope so, because this section is all about that message. Let's just take a moment to breathe…

Take a deep breath in… HOLD IT for 1…2…3…4…5, EXHALE…now try that again.

And again. And again…

Okay, you are now a little bit more grounded and back in the moment, so let's talk EMOTIONAL ATTACHMENT TO YOUR BUSINESS.

Being emotionally attached to your business can be a vibe killer, but you know that don't you. It's hard to detach as a heart centred soul. Truth is, it's BS like this in our minds that keeps us stuck and not being able to level up. Marketing is absolutely one of the areas levelling up requires some courage and grit. However, once you've got over the first hurdle, you'll find yourself in a better position and your confidence will continue to expand. That's the muscle to grow more of. Then your inner rebel can finally step up and get your freaking creative badge of honour on.

If you are anything like me and your neurodivergent brain spins at 20,000 miles per minute, then please note: this is going to be the most fun part of this journey in building your successful, soul aligned marketing strategy.

It really is as simple as plugin into subliminal (make sure they are wealthy ones BTW) and let your creative juices flow. The more your creative juices flow, the more empowered and rebellious you can be. The more powerful your message will be in your content and visibile within your branding.

How you choose to market your business is your permission slip to be authentically you. What's more is, the more 'out there' you are with your messaging and content, the more magical your business will be.

It's literally a tried and tested tool… Stand out, be consistent and authenticity always wins.

I didn't have the courage for 'in your face' messaging / content creation for a long time. I just couldn't bring myself to stand out because it was scary AF. The thought of having to deal with other people's judgements, trolling and BS was just too much for me to deal with at the time.

Being good at marketing for others was always my strong point, being their biggest cheerleader and empowering them to move through the next level. It wasn't just a strong point; it was my natural way of being.

Before we begin crafting your messaging for your marketing, let's peek at your strengths!

What's your strongest point?

Are you a great cheerleader for others or yourself?

This is THE toughest part that my clients generally struggle with and whilst I hear them completely, I know it's time to level up. Being rescued is great but it doesn't resolve the issue.

Ever heard the phrase: "What you resist, persists?"

That's the phrase my mentor taught me and, to date, it's still true. Every time I dive deep into that space, am I resisting success? I come up with some magic answers.

Writing this book was a classic example for me. I started writing it in October 2022 and it's now November 2023 as I write this chapter and I only picked the writing back up again a few weeks ago.

Was it resistance? After all the procrastination I've done around this book, I now realise it's the toughest thing I've ever done.

What business activity is this book? MARKETING.

Why have I resisted it so much? It's my message, it's visibility and even though my conscious mind is saying yes let's do this, My SUBCONSCIOUS brain is saying NO WAY!

The difference between now and a year ago is I can now see the procrastination, whereas before, I was just focusing on other things and procrasti-eating to oblivion. Soon, real-life shizzle got in the way and I lost my mojo.

In 2023, it was a full shit show, but I reclaimed my power and said my famous last words on the topic:

"Fuck this shit, I'm ready for more!"

Building resilience isn't always easy, but working through it is always worth it.

I've learnt to detach from the emotional aspect of procrastination, so now, it's water off a duck's back. Resilience is key to rising above it all and moving your business to the next level.

Now I've talked you through the madness of how emotions can hold you back, I'm hoping you will take a little magical phrase away with you. Every time you notice yourself procrastinating, just repeat the following (or a similar phrase):

"Fuck this shit, I'm ready for more!"

Make a conscious decision to overcome the emotional hurdles and find your key to moving through it.

Every time I've made big decisions in my life; it's been when I have said that phrase and damn well meant it, through every single cell and fibre of my being.

We can tame it slightly if you like: "I reclaim my power and take action now!" or have a play with words and find your power phrase so you can BE exactly who you were always meant to be.

Now you've overcome that, it's time to get your message clear... LOUD AND CLEAR.

First, let's craft an introductory statement that your dreamy clients will be able to connect with you:

Step 1: I HELP / TEACH / SUPPORT/ EMPOWER CREATE

Choose a word to describe how you work with your dream client.

Step 2: Insert your dream client

Step 3: TO...

In this step, you are explaining what you help them achieve.

Step 4: So that...

Insert their desired outcome

EXAMPLE:

"I help spiritual entrepreneurs to create soul aligned offers, so they can generate consistent 5-figure months."

This is now a statement that enables my dream client to know what I do and how I can help them, but is that enough? NOPE!

When I read that statement for my business, I don't feel excited, powerful or ready to share my message. It's just a statement that I can throw out into the world and hope that something will come from it. It's not really aligned as I don't feel lit up with it. Something is missing. More specifically, it is my energy is that's missing. So, here's another lesson for you in marketing your business with your message. Your energy needs to flow with it so brightly with confidence, self-belief and comfort all rolled into one.

However, if you don't have that feeling straight away, don't worry because it's all a work in progress. You can make a start and perfect it as you go!

You can only learn and move; as you evolve in your journey, so does your message and this is the magic of you. Nothing stays the same for too long. Allow yourself to flow with the changes as they come, but always be conscious of the fact that to be fully in alignment, it's something to revisit on a regular basis.

Ultimately, your marketing message needs to be clear, powerful, strong and EMBODIED. Clients will sniff out a lack of confidence with you, so embody the confidence you have and grow that muscle regularly.

Updated example statement:

> "I teach gifted spiritual entrepreneurs to create more money & time freedom doing what they love, by crafting soul aligned offers, and energetically transforming their soul."

It's got a little bit more juice to that and all that happened was a play on words with:

> The best way I support my clients to achieve their desire, and how I do it.

Another uplevel would be:

> "I support the rebel soulpreneur to cultivate their 5-figure offers for ease and flow in their business. I do this so they can break free from cookie cutter strategies and own their gifts."

Once you have your **'STATEMENT'** that's powerful and showcases your essence, this is where the magic then begins.

Many people will follow a systematic approach to niching… I teach you to feel into your soul's desires and look at the dreamy client you want to work with, then craft your statement.

Dreamy clients are easier to get in alignment with, as you feel into what they need / desire and how you are the best person to serve them. We covered most of this in Chapter 2, so you can go back and revisit as many times as you need / want.

Moving on: what does a strong marketing message look like? A story... it is one that your dreamy client NEEDS to hear to HELP them achieve their DESIRE.

Statement / Hook / Title:

YOU DON'T NEED TO BE AN EXPERT TO GET STARTED WITH YOUR SPIRITUAL JOURNEY:

Insert opinion / views:

Many people believe they must have it all 100% perfected to get started. This is a huge misconception and the cause of procrasti-starting... Perfectionism won't get you where you want to be.

Insert EXPERIENCE:

In my years as an expert in my field, I've helped hundreds and thousands of spiritual entrepreneurs to cultivate their next level success, by working through their self-perceptions and limiting beliefs. I help them gainclarity over who they are and how they have got to where they are today. Most of which all started with this common belief that they have to be an expert to get started.

Insert truth:

All you need is confidence, knowledge, self-belief and experience in what you are wanting to get started with. On occasions, you don't even need that except a willingness to learn, train and move into the direction you want to travel in, so you can begin the journey.

Remember everything starts from one step, so take one step today and another one tomorrow.

Insert Client Story:

My client last week was struggling to formulate her plan. She was feeling lost and consumed with anxiety, believing she needed to be more than she was to cultivate the power within to act for what she wanted.

Together, we worked through her beliefs and now she has a magical dream plan of aligned actions, and a powerful message to share with her soul aligned dreamy clients.

Then invite them to chat with you, with a call to action.

If you are ready to get out of your own way, alchemise your beliefs and energy, get into alignment for your next steps, then send me a message to chat or book a free call.

The marketing message is an opportunity to showcase your skills, share your magic and cultivate a strong heart centred connection with your ideal client.

Give it a try and see how you get on. If you are already a seasoned entrepreneur, then let's go back to your message and infuse it with a little more confidence, power and knowledge than you have before.

Level it up! Be the expert, the knowledge, the power, the teacher, the mentor, the business owner.

If you do this regularly, you will shine beyond your expectations, grow your audience, create more sales, simplify your business and be more at peace with the life you are creating.

It's time to shine but don't just shine — get the fuck out there and do what you set out to do. Be the change maker, thought leader and empowered spiritual entrepreneur you know you are.

This leads us to the next part of your marketing: The Strategy!

You can't show up in your marketing if you don't have a strategy of where you want to be seen!

Pick your platforms. Keep in mind that marketing is so much more than just social media,: it's the media, podcasts, blogging, lead magnets and so much more.

I don't recommend you hit them all though as that will send you down a rabbit hole of emptiness faster than procrastination. Not cool nor fun!

Talking of fun, what kind of ways do you like to consume marketing?

Do you prefer to read blogs? Watch videos on YouTube? Check out your competitors on social media? Listen to the radio?

Marketing your business needs to feel fun, empowering and most of all in alignment.

Here's some things you can do to get into alignment with your marketing:

1. DO MARKET RESEARCH WITH DREAMY CLIENTS - do not sell on that call! EVER
2. Connect with where **you** want to be seen
3. Think about PR
4. Where is your best online and offline presence - feel into it
5. Research Keywords
6. Check out your competitors (do not copy) - Keep it ethical and inspirational for your own creative juices to flow

Most of all, don't let RESISTANCE be the killer of your business before you've even begun. Clear the resistance or work through it then decide if it's an alignment thing or not.

Remember **Marketing = Manifesting**
= bring your dreams alive!

NOTE

CHAPTER 8

Unlock Abundant Sales Your Way

Hate sales? Does it feel icky? Are you afraid of the 'ickiness? Does it literally make your body respond in an uncomfortable way?

Okay. I'm not going to beat around the bush here; it's just time to change the trajectory. The story your mind is feeding you around sales is utter BS... **SALES = ENERGY EXCHANGE OF VALUE.** What is an energy exchange? It's where you give something and you receive something in return.

It's your time to be the true leader of your life's purpose and being of SERVICE.

Now, let's think about that: to be of service means you create impact and change in the world around you, helping others, whilst feeling needed, wanted, valued and supported.

People serve people. However, in today's society of 2024 and beyond, we are no longer living in a world of giving and exchanging energy: we have a new currency.

You may, as a spiritual entrepreneur, begin to feel very uncomfortable with this vibration that is coming in.

But wait… this isn't just a vibration. Deep in your soul, this is more than that. Deep in your subconscious is a story of energy exchanges, worthlessness and trauma from experiences that make you feel uncomfortable with the word sale, the energy of receiving money and putting yourself out there to 'sell'.

This is what causes most of the spiritual entrepreneurs I've worked with to not like the energy of sales — past traumas around the word sales and money.

Money is felt deep in your heart's core as a negative thing that people of power have used for bad things. Well, I'm sorry to tell you but that hasn't changed in the world completely yet. However, it doesn't mean that you have to continue this charade of old programming and storytelling.

When it comes to money and sales, the energy is the same, yet so different. HERE IS MY PERSONAL TAKE ON THE ENERGY of MONEY and Sales.

The energy of Money = Unconditional LOVE and Acceptance from self and others

The energy of Sales = Abandonment and Rejection

Read that again… The energy of money is based around self-love and love from others = unconditional love, openly receiving with ease.

Sales = Fear of abandonment & rejection, putting up walls and barriers to success.

How you **FEEL** about sales and money is not the reality.

It's the same principle with how you think, behave and respond to it. The connection you have to the word sales or money is the story that has been keeping you stuck in a loop and hard to breakthrough to new levels.

I want to explain the emotional connection to sales before we move on, because it's really important you become radically aligned to your own sales process and aware of your money mindset. It impacts your business, more than you realise.

Of course, there are businesses that are not impacted in those energy exchange processes; those businesses are usually corporate and led by everyone else but the owner.

I'm going to assume you are not the owner of a corporate company, but a genuine heart and soul led spiritual entrepreneur who just wants to serve the world, be a changemaker and help people.

(humour me!)

The parts of you that are not about the money and just want to serve leaves you and your bank balance juggling the money pot, to survive. You end up constantly moving money around to cope and then you end up borrowing. All whilst sitting back and thinking it's okay because the universe has got your back and it won't always be this way.

Fast forward 4,5,10+ years… the story hasn't changed. You are still serving from a heart centred place and still chasing the money in small quantities, trusting that the universe has got your back.

It is cool that you listen to that inner wisdom, but you also know deep down that this isn't the reality you wanted for yourself. However, it's okay because you are a heart centred leader and it's not about the money… right?!

How about no! How about your sales and money mindset need a shake up!

This is not OK.

Please, with every inch of me, can I please ask you to stop this cycle for yourself and others. **Please… Stop this now!** Our future generations need this pattern to be cleared so they can rise into the spiritual space and create wealth, removing poverty and making a massive impact in the world globally.

Everything I have explained above is the reality of heart centred leaders worldwide. Money and sales mindset in business is crucial, not just for survival but for your own self-esteem, confidence and to reach those dreams.

Therefore, how you feel about the word sale and the energy of money will dictate the level of success you receive if you let it. This is something I'm deeply passionate about. At first, I was everything in that previous description and more. Rather than allowing myself to receive all I deserved, I would reject the abundance coming at me. I didn't see myself as worthy, so creating sales was a nightmare.

Working on my money and sales mindset energetically was a game changer. Manifesting my desires was also a game changer.

The one shift I really needed was to open my heart to receiving. Knowing it was safe to receive, ask and dream bigger than ever before.

It took me a lot of practice and deep inner work, but it made all the difference when I began receiving worthy payments for my work. It gave me time back to be who I wanted to be without working my fingers to the bone.

Creating an income gives you more than financial stability in the here and now; it helps you create generational wealth and the ability to serve more people.

Think about that mission you have to serve others in need. Perhaps you want to support an animal sanctuary or a charity. Just think of all the good you can do when you have the extra pockets of cash!

Money and Sales are a good thing. If you can see through that, you will start changing your story. Little by little, day by day.

Okay... I think we have covered enough around the energy, beliefs and programming of sales and money. Nowlet's move the needle and begin something different.

Place your hands on your heart and ask yourself this: how much do you really want to earn income wise?

Trust in the number that is given to you.

This is what we call aligned pricing.

The next step is to look at your offers/products/services: can you confidently navigate the dream income with that figure?

Yes? Awesome...

Let's bring the strategy in!

Sales and Money mindset are only one aspect of the business growth game. You will also need aligned pricing and strategic pricing to reach your goal.

But how do you bring it all together to craft your soul aligned sales strategy?

This is where it gets a bit tricky.

Your intuitive guidance is probably being overshadowed with logic and of course ego, placing you into the depths of internal conflict.

Your business needs you to let go of your ego and trust in that inner wisdom.

Reverse engineer your goals.

Start with that dream income and now break it down into tangible steps, being intuitive, creative, joyful and find easy to execute your sales strategy with love - knowing this:

EVERY SINGLE PERSON YOU INVITE TO BE A CUSTOMER IS ANOTHER PERSON YOU HAVE MADE AN IMPACT WITH.

- Your sales strategy, when done well, becomes the invitation to the heart and soul of your ideal client.
- Your sales strategy is your client's invitation to resolve a problem.
- Your sales strategy is best coming from your way of doing things.

If you were to invite a client to work with you, how would you like to do that? What would you like to say? How would you like them to respond? Where will they find you? What is their best way to pay you? Why are they chomping at the bit to throw money at you?

Go and play. Answer these questions, find YOUR way of inviting your dream client to work with you, then build upon that strategy! Make it work for you.

NOTE

CHAPTER 9

Being Magnetic, Planning and Action

Client attraction through law of attraction: have you tried that method? It's referred to as attraction marketing.

Attraction marketing can be hot and spicy or gentle and loving. Either way, it's like rubbing the lamp of the genie and watching your business unfold - just like magic.

There are times, however, that attraction marketing doesn't work in the way you want it to. This is when business feels a little sticky and shite.

Picture yourself now trying to swim through treacle... Definitely not going to be easy, right? Of course not. It's going to be one of those crappy days where Alannis Morisette starts with her power ballad: Ironic!

So, the questions then begin. How can you step into attraction marketing and call your soul aligned clients to you through your content and marketing strategies?

No, before you think it, it's not a magic wand situation here! Get that thought out of your head now. It's in the energy behind your goal and soul aligned offer... pricing and messaging. A recipe is soon forming.

I won't tell you how many training courses and programmes I've bought over the years on marketing and writing. It's embarrassing! BUT...This level of commitment has given me some clear tips to help you unlock your next bit of success and learn your own way of creating attraction marketing in your business.

The most engaging pieces are those that come from your heart space of talking to your ideal client who you talk to everyday, knowing EXACTLY what they need, why they need it and how you can best serve them. You don't just talk to them as numbers or as I say 'like pie in the sky'... you talk to their soul. A bit like me writing this to you now. I know you want to actively move that needle in your business, you want to uplevel and that's why you're reading this book. You want success... You want dreams... You want goals and have desires. You want to learn more.

The thing is, you possess all of that! You may have just forgotten the power you have within to create it.

This is where I come in... Your ability to connect with attraction marketing is your soul connecting to your aligned clients and customers. It's a feeling — an energy and a deep connection to truth. When you are Radically Aligned to your business, the foundations and the attraction from soul aligned clients embodies it all. In turn it creates positive results for you and your client.

Many entrepreneurs get stuck on a mission of discontentment and allow the energy of lack and scarcity to put them into fight / flight / freeze. However, this generally creates hustle mode and shows up in energy in their marketing and content.

Unfortunately, hustle energy is impacting your ability to attract soul aligned clients. Your energy is collected from your desire and belief. You attract all that you are energetically matched to. This is why your attraction marketing journey feels like swimming through treacle sometimes. The thing about this type of marketing is your energy dictates the outcome: your belief systems match the vibration of the client you are communicating with.

It's also an opportunity for you to learn more about who you are, what you are allowing into your life and who you desire to be.

Here's an example: You want a high-end client to pay £20k+ for 6 months' work. You tell the universe with unshakeable conviction that this is what you are going for, yet your messaging is small, your language is soft, your confidence is low, and you don't believe for one minute you can do this.

You fight against it, you push through, you create 6 months' worth of content and for the first 3 months, all you hear is crickets.

This is your learning curve with the law of attraction and attraction marketing!

You must believe in your ability to connect and achieve your goal / dreams. It means that anything out of alignment will have a negative effect. This is where most people get stuck with crafting content that stipulates attraction marketing.

You now have a choice to choose again and do things differently.

To tap into your **TRUTH** about the goals, offers, language, trust, beliefs and structures of your business, here's a starting point for how we do that!

Step 1: Tune into how you really feel about your offer, pricing structure and messaging.

What's the negative aspect of your thoughts? What's positive?

Is the language in alignment with you, your goal and your client?

Example: My client is excited to finally smash those upper glass ceilings, so they achieve success limitlessly.

This level of communication has a splash of confidence and belief but also connects to my client's soul of desires.

The pain the client has already experienced such as frustration, disconnect and fear are not something they want to focus on.

Attraction marketing speaks into existence what is desired for you and your clients. You basically become a storyteller. So, let's just say my client, Deirdre, wants a 10K month to start her journey to becoming a 7-figure business owner, yet she's currently only turning over £3k months:

Here is a clear example of attraction marketing:

Looking at the window, scratching your head and dreaming of the results of your 10K+ months? You've got your plan, experience, gifts, existing clients and your offer is potent AF.

You've done it alland now you are ready for more. You are ready for soul activated, embodied success of trust, liberation, truth and discernment. You are fearlessly captivated in the knowing of what you can achieve. You are ready to:

- Feel connected
- Take action
- Step into success
- Break through glass ceilings
- Overcome the inner critic
- Achieve your desires

You know that with the right support and guidance, your next level is going to be abundant and strategically aligned. All you need now is the support to make it happen (Insert a story as to how you overcame this and achieved your success)

THEN you would insert your programme / offer promised. Let's break it down:

Section 1: This piece is talking to the client who DOES THIS:

Looking at the window, scratching your head and dreaming of the results of your 10K+ months? You've got your plan, experience, gifts, existing clients and your offer is potent AF.

Section 2: This piece talks about all they have completed so far: You've done it all… got the foundations, and now you are ready for more.

Section 3: This piece explains how they feel about moving forward:

You are ready for soul activated embodied success of trust, liberation, truth and discernment. (Insert a story as to how you overcame this and achieved your success)

You are fearlessly captivated in the knowing of what you can achieve and you are ready to:

- Feel connected
- Take action
- Step into success

- Break through glass ceilings
- Overcome the inner critic
- Achieve your desires

Section 4: Understanding what they need now:

You know with the right support and guidance that your next level is going to be abundant AF and strategically aligned. All you need now is the support to make it happen.

Section 5: Inviting them into your world with an appropriate call to action.

Constructing attraction marketing is also about ensuring you are talking about your existing clients by using story-based results from case studies, as an example. You are now showcasing the work you do without having to say it! Just like sharing testimonials which attract clients too!

However, the pieces of content you write have to come from a heart centred space. Trust and believe in what you do so your soul aligned dream clients can find you and connect with you.

It's time to elevate… act now to become radically aligned and step into attraction marketing.

1. Clear away any doubts, fears and uncertainties. Be very honest with how you feel about ALL of this, DAILY! How you feel about your success is what will create the success. It's an energetic mind workout that is required daily.

2. Embody the success that is required, bring the nervous system up to date with the safety and stabilisation of receiving, holding and having all you have ever dreamt of. Embodiment brings clarity and confidence.
3. Is connecting with your language empowering? Disempowering? Engaging? Rejecting? Focus on the energy you want your client to receive and let the language you share match that vibration.
4. Are you sharing from a space of love and growth orr lack and scarcity? Be mindful of what you are sharing in your content.
5. Awaken your heart chakra and allow yourself to receive more. The more you can receive, the more empowered your journey to success will be.
6. Write content and marketing pieces with your client's journey in mind. You know your clients' needs more than they do, remember that. They are coming to you as the expert but be mindful of how you can accommodate their journey in preparation to receive your expertise.

Your energy attracts and repels, much like your vibration and words. It's not a one time fix but a consistent journey of internal growth and expansion.

Think about your soul aligned embodied success. When you are open to receiving and it feels safe, you will receive with love. When you are in doubt, fear or lack of trust, it will be challenging to achieve your goals.

If you want to go deeper, I've recorded a 24-minute clearing and embodiment activation for £20k+ months.

Using Coupon Code: **BookGift1**

Scan the QR Code below to grab yours

Or go to: www.vickichisholm.com/radically-aligned .

Use the notes pages to help guide you through the journaling after you have completed the audio.

NOTE

CHAPTER 10

Committing to Your Success

Don't tell me you want success then go on to do 100 x other things that distract you... Resistance is futile, as my mentor shared with me. She also went on to say:

"Vicki, what you resist, will persist." Yep that was me officially screwed from hiding behind my own juicy BS of life. It was time to wake TF up and decide whether to continue a pattern or face my inner demons and work through it.

But you, as an unbelievably amazing, beautiful soul, possibly have something in your brain similar to me:

A neuro-spicy, crazy AF magpie for all things magical and abundant!

Yeah? Agreed?

We live in a world where focus is no longer our priority. Now, if you get me, you get me: if you don't, you don't. I'm just here to share my wisdom and explain a little about this thing called Neuro-whacky (MY PERSONAL CHOICE OF WORDS) brain cells, AKA ADHD (Attention Deficit Hyperactivity Disorder)

If you experience (not suffer) a million ideas a day, super ambitious, creative AF and just love all things related to all things, the chances are as an entrepreneur you may have a little thing called ADHD... You may not.. but either, the bottom line is that it doesn't matter.

Now... let's just throw a tiny little spanner in the works here.

You are reading my book and that could be because you also have a splash of woo woo spiritual connection tapped into your brain's processing... (In case you didn't know, most people do but not all people accept that though).

Whilst it's not your fault for being distracted at all, it just means we have other avenues to cover such as being grounded and not allowing the 'downloads' to consume you.

When you are grounded, you are in a space of self-connection, safety and regulation. On the other hand, when you are not grounded, your brain flies off to the moon and brings back aliens which forces you to social media scroll until, in 10 seconds flat, you have just forgotten the task at hand.

Oh yes... This is the entrepreneurial brain: distraction and ambition all rolled into one. Social media, kids, phones and external noise all impacts your ability to focus on what you want.

The difference is, you and only you can be the one who decides to break the distracted patterns or not as these are habits.

Now let's talk about commitment to yourself. It's the most self-loving thing you can do. EVER.

Often, I see clients who will say, "Why won't they commit to me?" in relation to their own clients and relationships. They don't normally focus on commitment to themselves.

When you are not committing to yourself, you are vibrating with uneven energy. So, you will begin to attract uneven vibrational matches.

When you 100% commit to yourself, the world will match that. It's not easy at all but it is all in the experience of who you are and what you achieve.

Self-commitment is when you choose to invest in programmes, courses, coaching, healing and any form of health and wellness for growth and empowerment.

As a coach myself but also a participant, I've witnessed both sides of the experiences. The truth is, if you didn't get results with one coach or pro- gramme, there is no blame or shame to be had. It's an experience that both you and your coach have to go through to get you to the other side.

I've had to learn this the hard way. I was stuck in resistance and couldn't break through but instead of chipping away at the layers presenting to me, I was 'feeling' that the path in front of me was misaligned.

I felt burnt at the fingers where I believed promises were made and I didn't get the results, so instead of working through the issues at hand, I kept jumping from coach to coach, mentor to mentor, programme to programme and course to course. FOR YEARS, I didn't have the knowledge or strength to overcome the resistance back then.

I've also witnessed the same energy in some of my clients... Instead of acknowledging and working through their layers, they choose to quit, not fully commit and blame me and the programme and everything else in between.

If it wasn't for my other clients who are soul aligned, and activated a joy to work with, the chances are I probably wouldn't be in business now... I want my clients to succeed. I absolutely do and this is why aligned clients are way more joyful to work with than those who are not ready for you!

The thing is, if you continue with the same story from one course / programme / coach to the other, then there is a subconscious block keeping you stuck and that's where you need to do the work to get on track. It's not your fault and it's not your coach's fault. It's also not the programme's fault as there are many factors in the process. Please though, for the sake of your own sanity, forgive the process and experience, look deeper at the matter in hand and move through it.

Forgiveness is the key to help you move beyond this situation.

Always remember that commitment to self will save you time, money and energy... EVERY TIME.

It means not giving up, not throwing in the towel and not creating a victim mindset.

Cool we got that bit out of the way, so let's look at the next step...

Self-commitment to your goals, dreams and ambitions. Noone else can achieve your dreams / goals. It's all down to you!

You are the catalyst of success: your coach, mentors, training and guides are all here to support and help you navigate

the path, but **only you** can be the driving force of your commitment to your desires.

Throughout this book, we have spoken of many things: energy, mindset, strategy, marketing, alignment, messaging, connection, growth, offers and success. Yet all of that is based on you COMMITTING to what you want, doing the work and choosing to learn along the way. That

This is the real hard nugget of truth section: are you fully into your success or are you half-assing it?

Be honest with your answers here because the only one that gets truly cheated by lack of honesty is you.

Let's go back to testing your truth in the what you want section: Are you fully committed to your goals / dreams and desires here? Are they 100% fully charged with your inner magic?

Feel into your heart space on a scale of 0-10 how committed are you to this vision?

0 = Not committed at all - low vibe - what's the point energy
10 = I'm all in… watch me smash this

If it's less than 10… there is work to do.

If it's less than 7, the resistance may be too big

If it's less than 5, go back to the drawing board and reconsider what it is you do want.

Now, do the same for each section:

- Your ideal dreamy client: are they the most aligned to you? How easy is it going to be for you to reach them?
- Your soul aligned offer: Are you excited to share it with your dream client? Does your client want to bite your hand off for it?

- Are you ready to show up every day and share your offer with those who need you?
- Your pricing: Does it feel good? Are you 110% confident that the price is correct?
- Your marketing message is confident AF and bursting at the seams with magical content. Do you feel excited to navigate your marketing platforms of choice?
- Are you ready to move forward and make this your most amazing successful launch ever?
- Have you crafted your next steps plan? Does that feel good?

Notice any spaces where you are not in aligned movement and make some decisions about who you need support from and what actions come next.

Do you need accountability? Support? Empowerment? Delegation? What are your weak areas and where are your strengths?

Committing to yourself isn't about playing the martyr; it's all about committing to the journey and knowing what you want, need and how to bring it all together.

This is where my clients usually jump into my radical realignment 1:1 programme, so they can fully have that support to move through the disconnected states of resistance and unlock the mystery of misalignment. Align to their goals, business and true soul aligned success.

Remember what we said earlier about misalignment is not knowing that something is missing, and resistance is the fear that creates stories of disempowerment?

TWO VERY DIFFERENT ENERGIES ALL TOGETHER.

NOTE

CHAPTER 11

Fast Track Your Way To Success

In case you skipped the entirety of this book to get to the juicy bits, I have a little something for you…

Reality Check.

GO BACK AND READ THE CONTENTS…

You absolutely cannot skip the juicy details and fly your way to the top of the mountain without some seriously amazing ingredients…

The ingredients for you to fast track your success are made of smaller details that require you to take some action and NOT SKIP ALL THE JUICY BITS of the recipe.

Well, you can, but you won't get the full benefit…

The fast track is a magical resource that allows you to create flow with clarity, knowledge, belief and certainty.

You can fasttrack your success when you have the recipe nailed and your confidence rocket launched.

That is a fact.

Look at those super-duper marketers out there killing it. They use their skills to market their offerings and sell like superstar selling queens / kings. In fact, they sell without selling! Ever noticed that? Go back to attraction marketing in chapter 9 ... it's a real thing, you know.

Anywho, you may be thinking how do these people get results. Well, it's a simple recipe... all you have to do is craft it to your own delight, whisk up your soul aligned contents and find your clarity for what you truly desire.

There are reasons and experiences why this may not be happening exactly how you want it right now, but trust me when I say, you can and will succeed in the greatest of delights.

I teach my clients a process, the radically aligned, fasttrack process.

The process allows you to finally fall into alignment for all that you are and all that you desire to do...

It ia a recipe you can rinse and repeat to your advantage, every SINGLE DAY.

It all starts with these 6 steps:

1. Know what you want
2. Know who you want to serve
3. Know your offer
4. Know your pricing
5. Know your message, marketing & Sales
6. Know your client journey

As you navigate the movements between these 6 steps, instead of jumping around like a crazy person wondering if this is the right time or moment for you, it's time to switch up the energetics, beliefs and structure of all you desire.

Inside each of the six steps I teach you (navigated throughout this book), the energies, the way you think and feel, and flow is what will structure your success.

The fast-track business accelerator programme I created is to ensure you are doing the inner work alongside your **own** crafted success in building your radically aligned business.

Now, I have had clients make amazing outcomes from this process and I've had clients STRUGGLE through this process.

What is the difference between this process winning and this process falling you may ask? THE CLIENT is the difference. I've had clients who are super confident in what they do but just needed a shift in focus to achieve their outcomes.

I've then had clients who have refused to follow their inner guidance and truth, allowed resistance to get in the way and stop them succeeding.

This was my learning curve that not everyone is ready for soul aligned success. This was also a painful experience in my world as a coach / healer and something I had to learn. I want EVERYONE to succeed, especially gifted spiritual entrepreneurs who are changing the world.

If you are not ready for soul aligned success, this process will be a struggle, but if you are ready to do the inner work and listen to your inner guidance to flow into alignment and craft your most magical business ever, then I welcome you to dive in and go for the fast track option. Do the steps! Download my free guide to take you there.

In fact, I challenge you to rinse and repeat this process until you succeed! Go through your own journey of the fast track and find yourself, be who you really are, do what you truly want and flow into all you know you can be.

You see, radically aligned success all starts with you... your ability to gain your own truth, listen to what you desire and take aligned action.

Radically aligned means you have decided to connect with your soul, follow what you wanted and let the external noise dissipate. Being in a state of radical alignment will enable you to be the leader and the go to specialist in your field. You have to be ready for that.

Radical alignment to your business allows you to step away from being told what you need and what you MUST do by others and teaches you to follow your own inner compass of what is YOUR SOUL ALIGNED PATH.

It teaches you to turn up the dial of your own mission and stand with unshakeable conviction in trusting where you are, who you are and where you are going to be.

The fast-track process is just that: a process to enable you to find your truth and build a business that flows in the way you want it to.

I'm a little tired of the online space and noise that makes you feel misunderstood, alone and afraid to show up as you are and how you truly want to be.

I want to see more soul aligned success unfold, in the way it is supposed to for YOU - not your coach, your mentor or your teacher.

>>>> **YOU** <<<<

Your business, your offers, your clients, your experience, YOUR WAY.

Your gifts and magic need you to step into your truth!

Choose radical alignment of truth, self-trust and contentment as it will lead you to always have what you need / desire in your life and business.

What do you have to lose for diving deep into soul aligned business success? Nothing!

What do you have to gain?

You have **EVERYTHING** to **GAIN**.

The Fast Track to business success and becoming radically aligned is yours; you just have to decide it's what you want and then create your soul aligned strategy to get you there.

My mission is to see you succeed… but I bring you to answer this question now:

Am I ready to step into soul aligned business success?

Sit with this, feel into this and awaken your truth, so you can have the answers from within to navigate your next steps to success.

NOTE

Final Thoughts

Final Thoughts for your ongoing journey for a radically aligned business:

Put into practice the teachings and remember you don't have to run your business the way others tell you too. The magic and power is the way you decide to craft it.

How can I help you do that? Well, let me introduce you to my world where you can consider the next steps… by feeling into what you need and how working together can help you expand your soul aligned business success.

Check out the resources and ways in which we can work together on the pages over leaf.

Before you go to explore, follow me on social.

Take a selfie with this book and tag me!

THE RADICALLY ALIGNED 1:1 BUSINESS INTENSIVE™

Wanna be a VIP? Radically Aligned 1:1 Business Intensive, this is one of my favourite services to date. It's a 6-week container to spruce up your business and energetically realign you to what you do want.

We bespokely craft your radically aligned business from your soul. That's right. I take you back to who you truly are. Awaken the light within you and support you to bring your business and life back together.

It's not for the faint hearted, and you will experience deep transformational work, as we navigate your inner desires and bring them to life, through soul aligned strategy. **This is for the seasoned spiritual entrepreneur who feels a lack of clarity and disconnect to bring the business back to life through realignment and strategy. It's a business boost from the inside out.**

THE FAST TRACK BUSINESS ACCELERATOR 2.0™

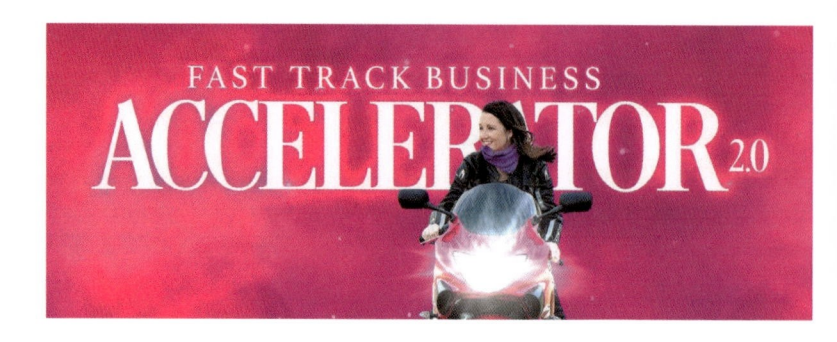

Do you like to have group settings as well as 1:1 personalised support? Join me inside the Fast Track Business Accelerator 2.0... My signature programme is specifically tailored to bring the magic of a group coaching package together with personalised 1:1 support.

This 6-month programme is a hybrid opportunity to bring your magic to the world around you, inside your business, inside yourself and build lifelong relationships from those you are masterminding with.

I'm not here for the surface level mind fuckery... let's go deep into your transformation and build your business your way!

This is for the spiritual entrepreneur who have a business and already onboarding clients, have 4-5 figure inconsistent months, and ready to activate the next level to multi- five figure months, by gaining clarity, insight and soul alignment to business and self, over a 6-month period. This container comes with a guarantee, if you don't reach your desired journey within the 6 months, we extend your time inside the programme until you do!

RADICALLY ALIGNED BUSINESS STRATEGY & BREAKTHROUGH SESSION™

This is a one-off session, where you and I will spend one hour on your energetics and strategic alignment for growth… expansion in ONE area of your business that is disconnected. These sessions are POWERFUL AF, and I would highly recommend as a starting point.

The Growth Academy Online Membership:

Weekly group coaching calls for energetic sales and money mindset, this is the first base for those who are not reaching their income goals and are open to combining Energy & Sales for their next level.

Life Changing Self-Help Courses

28 DAYS to Personal Power Programme:

This is a life changing self-help programme that enables you to craft a daily routine and reclaim your power for success in all areas of life and business. This 28-day experience is filled with 5-10minutes of EFT every day for you to follow along with, which includes a reclaim your power PDF journal, tapping out the blocks PDF and 2 additional audios to support your journey.

Additional Resources:

Scan the QR Code Below for more info

Feel free to go to:

https://vickichisholm.com/radically-aligned

for access to resources or reach out to me on the socials!!

Bonus points to you for taking a selfie with this book and sharing on the socials don't forget to tag me!

Book me as a Speaker / Trainer at your event

I'd love to speak for you and your audience, at an event, workshop, podcast or maybe even a summit, as a highly engaged down to earth, inspirational and motivational speaker / coach and all round badass global leader.

My topics are:

- Soul Aligned Business Success
- Crafting soul aligned offers
- Energy Transformation to reclaim your power
- Life After Domestic Abuse

Stages I have spoken on include: The Big Festoon hosted by Dani Wallace, where Lisa Maffia from So Solid Crew - one of my fave artists in my teens attended as a guest. I spoke alongside Lisa Johnson, Daniel Priestley, to name a few.

Testimonials

Andrea Rainsford From Women Winning In Business: "Vicki Chisholm is a powerhouse. A force of nature with a beautiful soul. She delivers her keynotes with passion and energy that knows no bounds. I knew I needed Vicki at my event to lift and inspire my audience. She will always be one of my keynotes of choice, because of her exceptional delivery and the passion for her craft"

Dani Wallace - Producer and Host of the Big Festoon "Vicki is a powerhouse speaker, her intuitive energy when speaking is such a skill when commanding the room. She delighted my audience at The BIG Festoon, providing, energy, thought provoking concepts and was a perfect addition to my line up. I can't recommend her highly enough!"

To book me as a speaker, please email:

admin@vickichisholm.com

Please be clear on what the event is, your dates / times / locations and topics you are looking to cover.

Thank you for reading all the way to the end.

Here's a little special shout out to everyone who has supported me on my journey from gutter to freedom.

Rachel Stone - Amazing Leadership Coach, Author and Speaker. Helen Pollock - Fabulous Book Coach & Speaker.

My family who has been on this wild journey with me, my friends, my neighbours, peers, clients, and mentors / trainers/ coaches – without you all, this book wouldn't exist.

Much Love to you all,

Vicki Chisholm

Printed in Great Britain
by Amazon